Angels and One Demon

A BOY CALLED RONNIE

COMING OF AGE

MY JOURNAL 1959-1968

D1737929

Author's Notes:

With utmost respect for the dignity and privacy of others, some of the names have been changed to ensure their anonymity and uphold their respect, reassuring readers that their personal stories are handled with care.

Embark on a transformative journey through the trilogy, starting with the innocence of a 4-year-old and progressing through the tumultuous years of adolescence. This first part sets the stage for the coming-of-age narrative that will captivate and resonate with readers of all ages.

The second part of the trilogy, a continuation of the chronological narrative, will delve into his life from ages 13 to 19.

The final book will cover the period from 19 years of age to the present.

ANGELS AND ONE DEMON-
" A boy called Ronnie."

This book is based on a true story of a boy looking, praying, and hoping for a change from the abusive life that was placed upon him. He blamed the government for major life-changing events he had no control over and sometimes felt like he was just collateral damage. At times, this child would turn his anger towards God, for he thought God was not listening or was too busy to answer his prayers. This boy also believes you may be blessed with angels when danger lurks in your footsteps. The story starts with an abusive father who was let out of the Army's mental institution in World War II. He was deemed mentally unstable by the United States Army medical doctors and was in the process of receiving electrical shocks to the brain. All that was required for his release was a simple signature for someone to take full responsibility for this person. This abused boy, approaching adolescence, was confused: lacking parental guidance, emotional support, and something called love. This is his story...

Author: Ronald E. Carpenter

© All rights reserved 2023

"angelsandonedemon@gmail.com"

ADDITIONAL INFORMATION ON BOOK'S CONTENTS

The book is about child abuse, neglect, and some unfortunate situations the child finds himself in. He was a confused child being mentored by believers in God and by the environment he grew up in.

Being poor, neglected, and abused will often come with a price tag. How much can a child endure before there is no recovery? This child also had a disability, which is now known as dyslexia. One may describe this book as "Coming of Age;" however, it is hard to put an actual label on one's life.

This book has been written, edited, and published by the author. There are no ghostwriters or fancy editors—just him, so feel free to get your red ink out.

This child eventually graduated high school but was last in his class and could not even write a sentence. His goal was to get that one piece of paper, and it was a high school diploma. This boy felt that if he couldn't do that, his life would feel meaningless, and he might become stranded in this world with no hope of a future. The boy had a fear that he might wind up becoming just like his abuser.

.

TABLE OF CONTENT

CHAPTER 1

UNCLE FRANKS RANCH

Today, the weather reminds me of a memory of a long time ago. I was a small child playing out in a yard, far from any city or worries that could distract a child of my age. I was happily playing with the things that God put on this earth for me to enjoy. There were lots of flowers and insects to play with and a large doghouse with no dog. I was at my dad's friend's ranch on the outskirts of Claremore, Oklahoma. My dad was standing on the front porch of Frank Vanhorn's Ranch- a man I called my uncle only out of respect, for he was not related by blood at all. My dad was staring up into the big, vast sky, which made this little fenced yard seem meaningless against the endless plains of rolling hills.

Just then, my Uncle Frank came out onto the front porch, a place that was the center of all family debates. My dad was still staring up into the sky when he opened another debate with a question. "Do you see those white and black clouds over yonder?"

My Uncle Frank's reaction to the question was implied by sucking on his teeth and scanning the huge clear blue sky. I was all ears by then because I had learned to grow and prosper by such debates. Most folks would say I had big ears like a jackrabbit, but I knew their remarks were just rubbish. Before my uncle could answer the question, my dad responded in his cocky tone of self-righteousness, saying, "The clouds that you see traveling towards each other will become a tornado."

My Uncle Frank looked back down at my dad, saying, "James, you don't know what you're talking about."

My Uncle Frank felt the same way I did. It looked impossible because the clouds were so small and so distilled in the outer atmosphere. Maybe my dad knew something we did not, or it was just a lucky prediction. It was a cold and a warm front approaching each other, and once again, it was time for tornado season to start. We lived on the Bible

Belt of this great land, but not without the absence of Satan's ungodly duels. The clouds came together and multiplied with such fury that all the living things upon the land stood as symbols of fear. Thunder and lightning raged as if an ungodly thing was present, seeking revenge on anyone or anything brave enough to stand in its way. We stood there as the rain's beginning turned quickly into the length of pencils before it hit the dry ground with its splat, releasing fragments of dry dust as its outer orbit. We were still standing there, for all of this came about within a few minutes as the conclusion to my father's vision turned into reality. A funnel appeared in the sky, and within the blink of an eye, it slapped itself down upon the dry land, knowing not what to destroy first.

It was like a hungry fox in a chicken coop, turning, twisting, and flying about. This twister turned its need for survival into nothing more than fun and games.

A call was made for the women folk to get into the cellar as my father sprang into the house after my mother. When we all had made it to the cellar, Dad noticed that I was frightened by lighting a candle and looking into my eyes. I was on the edge of peeing my pants. This oddly struck him as being funny, for he grunted at me, saying, "Would you like to see a tornado up close?" As usual, he did not give me a chance to reply. I was taken up the dirt steps of the cellar as he opened the door. The noise of the tornado's destructive power was incredible, and we saw the tornado as it was munching on the land. It looked as repulsive as one of my grasshoppers chewing at a dry piece of grass with his brown useless spit as a product of his contented efforts. Out of nowhere, a powerful frigid blast of wind ripped off the cellar door as if it were a gift to the ungodly thing. I looked up and saw the door was now an addition to the already flying elements of the circling winds. The winds pinned my father and me against the dirt collar door as my little legs dangled beside me. I could not hear what my dad was saying, but I could feel his vocal cords vibrate off my small back, and the smell of moonshine was overwhelming as it was exhaled from his lungs, moonshine that dad and my uncle would manufacture in the barn daily. My dad then lost his footing on the now muddy steps of the unprotected cellar.

As we fell to the bottom of the dusty, smelly hole, one of the women folks let out a yell that would bring you to your knees with repentance, asking God's forgiveness for any of your past sins. It was the black lady, Rose. The storm had detained her as she went farm to farm to collect washing and ironing to help pay for her children's way. When Rose laid out that incredible scream, she indeed paralyzed my heart. By yelling, "A spider! A spider!"

My mother, sitting next to her, lit a candle, and that was the most enormous black spider I had ever seen. My father went to take a gander at the big hairy thing and said, laughing. "Rose, damn! I was told black women can really scream!"

I was frightened, so I crawled under a bunk bed in a dry corner of the cellar floor, hoping it was a safe place to hide from the drunk. I stayed there until everyone had left the cellar. The house was still there when we emerged, but the wagon and the livestock were gone. I thought, now I know why my uncle has a doghouse but no dog.

The wagon was only a few paces north of the cellar, and unfortunately, a piece of the cellar went with it. My dad's way of removing fear was with the moonshine that he kept in his bottle. I was always afraid of my father because moonshine would clear his fear and remove his wits about right from wrong. I was, at times, the target for releasing his anger, as he'd hit and kick me if I did not act quickly enough on any of his commands. Some people would reference me as the little whipping boy. Dad would beat my mother more than me, and at times, she would have two black eyes. I remember that on some occasions, my mother would pack the car and drive for hours with my sister and me, then return to the same place she started from. She would hold her head low on the steering wheel, crying and saying, "I have no place to go." My mother was an orphan, and she had no other family except for my dad's. I was told my mother married my dad when she was only thirteen years old and lied about her age to do so. My dad was married once before, and his first wife disappeared in the middle of the night with their two boys because she feared for her life. She was fortunate because she had a family that could shelter them.

A week or so later, my father started to remodel the cellar. Dad must have felt a little guilty about what had happened to the door, as it led to the rainwater washing away the steps in that dark hole they call a cellar. After receiving permission from Uncle Frank by his customary grunts, we set off to go through things in the barn for items needed to rebuild that gofer hole. I always thought it was funny when my dad would grunt back at Uncle Frank as though he was mocking him, plus throwing in a few swear words that were always part of my dad's daily jargon.

After my Aunt Della prepared breakfast with her new, used wood-burning stove, my mother would help by doing the cleanup. Aunt Della was my Uncle Frank's wife, and my mother's name was uncommon and different from most folks. My Aunt Della would order Mother around the kitchen by saying, "Zola, you can do this, then try and do that!" Aunt Della treated my mother like a child, and she was not too far off in her thoughts.

We finally came to the barndoor, and it took some more grunts and swear words of unwisdom from my dad to open the swollen wooden door to one side. Once inside, we came across an old, damp couch that smelled musty and was so dirty I could barely see the flowers that had once been printed so boldly on it. My father grabbed the sofa and flipped it upright, pushing it towards the door. I noticed some movement on the ground from which this couch once came. I bent over with my hands stuffed into the pockets of my overalls so the items of interest I collected during the day would not fall out. It was baby field mice, so cute, warm, and full of new life.

That twister appeared again in that dusty, damp barn as it slapped upon that old dirt-filled floor, twisting, turning, and flying about. Small fragments of once-living things had just come to an end. This place, once meant for survival, was now just a blood bath of fun and games. I was still bent over as I slowly backed out toward the door with my now tightly fisted hands stuck in my pockets. I looked at my dad, who had feet like the twister, dancing, turning, and flying about. I dared not show any signs of fear, so I just put on a fake grin and ran back up to the house.

Sitting still in the corner of the kitchen, looking into the flames of the old wood-burning stove, my mind had questions about what I had just witnessed. My dad, at times, on his drunken spats, would do that same dance for me when he was whipping my mom. He would dance around me, pointing his fat finger at me, saying that I was not his son. He would preach to me in unbelievable anger, saying he came home and found my mom somehow had gotten pregnant.

My mom would always just lay close to the floor, crying and yelling at me not to listen to anything he would say. I remember those tantrums would go on for an hour or more, and Mother would get close to the floor, for she knew that was where she would always wind up. I would think to myself, if only mom had a gun, she could take care of this problem. This man was so full of anger and hate that I felt that someone needed to put him out of his misery. I knew if someone shot him, the problem would

17

come to an end, and I couldn't care less if this drunk died at my feet. There was no feeling of love or concern for me in this family, and I knew the thought of remorse at that time was not in my vocabulary. It seemed like many things were missing in my soul at that age, and I did not know what love was. I knew fear, hate, loneliness, and hunger for it were drilled into me at an early age. I would wake up knowing it was the same crap, just a different day.

CHAPTER 2

AUNT BETTY

It was Sunday morning again. I could always tell when I was awakened by Aunt Betty getting me undressed as I lay asleep on my one-mattress bed. Aunt Betty was Frank Vanhorn's daughter-in-law. She was a lovely lady who moved and glimmered like an angel. No matter where she went, the faith was with her. The big book of King James never strayed too far from her side. Every Sunday morning, she would drive out of her way to make sure I grew up proper. She felt like my soul always needed a good cleansing and made remarks like, "God only knows what goes on around here, and I know he's watching." I could always tell how disturbed she was at the men of the house by how she displayed sympathy for me. She would wake me, undress me, then stand me in a not-so-warm pale of water. She would always ask me questions about the marks on my back and legs. As always, I would tell her I got into a fight. In truth, my dad would attack me in his drunken rage, and I always did my best to come out on top. I would always fight back, but he sometimes won if I got myself cornered. Most of the time, I could get away by using one tactic or another, kicking his jollies or biting his leg. One time, when he got me in the corner, I almost bit off his thumb to escape. This drunk would always pass out after the fight, never remembering what happened when he woke up the next day. Well, that was at least what my mother would proclaim; however, the crazy drunk remembered he almost lost his thumb in a fight.

I remember one time I couldn't free myself, for he had me in a chokehold. I stood there taking it, yelling at him to get it over with by saying over and over, "Kill me! Just kill me!" Dad was so drunk he could barely stand up and couldn't continue and left me in my pool of tears. I felt so depressed, unhappy, lonely, and confused.

One time, I cut my face up using a razor blade, wondering if it would hurt if I just ended my life. Standing there in front of a mirror, bleeding, thinking about such things, was frightening me, and I started thinking, trying to find some reason to live. I was disturbed and confused about why my mother's mom hung herself. On top of that, some of my mom's kinfolk suffered the same faith. I thought to myself. Does this sickness run in the family? My mother's dad disappeared before my mother's mom decided to string herself up. It made my mother homeless at an early age, and the farmers who took her in abused her. Mom said she was never allowed to sit on the furniture and even had her special place at mealtimes in the corner of the floor.

My mother did not know how to protect me from my dad, nor did she even know how to protect herself. I thought about the ones that cut their life short. Could my life have been different if they had just stuck around and not been so selfish? That was the last time I thought about pulling my plug. I may wrongfully change the lives of others in such a wrong way. I felt heartbroken about their loss. If they had stuck around, they might have been able to open that door to the thing I was missing, which was a thing called love.

I believe this is why this lady, whom I called my Aunt Betty, stepped in. Perhaps she was guided to do so by an angel, or maybe she was one working undercover.

Sometimes, my Aunt Betty's questioning got a little embarrassing, like when asking me about

22

personal things as trying to find out at what point did this physical abuse stopped. One time, she smiled a little as she examined me, questioning me, and then popped off a remark saying, "I can see you're not Jewish."

In those days, the saying was if you brought your child into this world, you have the right to take them back out. Some folks wondered if this person I called Dad was even my father. There were rumors, and many things did not add up, like, for example, how you can marry a thirteen-year-old kid and not be divorced from the one who got away in the middle of the night. I hated my dad's first wife for doing so, and I did not even know her because now I had to deal with this crazy lunatic I now call Dad.

One Sunday morning, I could tell that something had fallen off the frying pan when my aunt grabbed the lye soap, scrubbing me repeatedly and not missing a spot.

I had to go to the outhouse but pledged I would never do what I did last Sunday, not ever again. When I returned from the outhouse last Sunday morning, I received a second washing on my bright red skin. I was always so dirty that I would proudly put a nice earthly ring around that old tin tub. Aunt

Betty stood beside the wood-burning stove to buff me off before I was clothed. I stood there in my shiny and clean overalls; in a way, I felt like I was being dislocated from my heritage of being dirty and mean. I stood there, gobbled up by her sizeable white dress, as she stood close to me, parting my ash-blond hair at the top of my head. She would bend over, hug me, and give me a slight kiss on the cheek, saying, "It's time to go; just follow me."

We got to the kitchen door, and she touched my head. It was her way of signaling me to stand, be quiet, and not even try to move. I stood in the doorway, knowing she was about to have it out with the men folks of the house on the things that were troubling her the most. I looked down at myself and felt a little embarrassed. I looked as clean as my Aunt Betty, who, to most people, was considered a saint. I stepped back around her large white dress so I could not be seen. I knew later the men folks of the house would be making fun of me.

She was upset about things lying in the yard and feared the owners would be coming looking for their belongings. My Uncle Frank's idea to keep the price up on his moonshine operation was to put others out of business. This old fart was a businessman, and he knew he had to cut down on the competition that may spoil his operation. He made the best moonshine known in these parts, proven to be of high quality, and was not the nasty crap that may blind you. My Uncle Frank's business was what one would say was well-established. Behind his old barn lay large piles of empty recycled jars that were necessary for his establishment, and at times, I would borrow one or two for my collection of bugs.

My Aunt Della told me that Greenhorns in the business tried to cancel out my uncle. They would do drive-by shootings upon his old wooden house, trying to put the fear of God into him; however, I knew my uncle did not know that person. My Aunt Betty had reason to be concerned and feared that I might become a target.

I did have an older sister who was a year older than me. She was out on loan to some other family; in those days, people would take care of children if they felt the parents were incapable of doing so. Most folks needed extra free help to help with the kitchen chores or to work out on the farm. In this land, you were there to work and help provide for the good of the family's unity. However, it seems to me being a drunken outlaw was an easier way to make a living.

After stepping back around the kitchen corner, I knew my aunt would unload the best of her wisdom. I could smell the sulfur burning as the words shot from her mouth. Maybe the smell could have been my dad's dirty socks he would heat up on the wood-burning stove. Aunt angrily asked her father-in-law and my dad if the ladies of the house knew exactly what was piled up outside. They could not answer back at her, for there is no escape when you're cornered by a saint.

My aunt grabbed the strap of my overalls and tried dragging me behind her. She tugged me so hard that the button of my overalls popped off to the floor. Then she quickly grabbed the last strap, which I needed to keep my pants up, so now I was voluntarily being dragged out. I started yelling out for help because I was being hijacked by a saint. My aunt did not think that was funny because I was clowning around. When we got out to her pickup truck, she told me, "Stop the crap, young man," and instructed me to step onto the broken starter button, which was relocated someplace on the floor as she was turning the key.

Maybe I better stop trying to be funny before I get my big mouth slap into a different day.

I did not wish to go to her church because they sometimes would speak in tongues; it was weird and, at times, frightened me. Maybe it's best if I did disappear today. Aunt Della was also afraid that some proprietors would come looking for the weasels that would strike at their goods in the night. I knew my Aunt Betty had three children and, for some reason, took a particular interest in me. Aunt Betty went to her place of worship, and her husband CJ went to his place along with his children.

The children were from CJ's first wife, who was raised in the Catholic faith, and my Aunt Betty was never previously married but was raised as Pentecostal.

Aunt Della told me that Catholic people could do as they wish and ask for forgiveness weekly when Pentecostal believers draw a line in the sand in hopes that the winds are not blowing too hard. My Aunt Della always had an opinion of people and how the world works. Aunt Della was well educated by studying what others had to say on the Radio.

When Aunt Betty hijacked me, my mother and Aunt Della were working long hours at the roadside café on the main highway. Mother was being instructed on how to become a waitress. Mother needed a way to provide for the family and knew my dad could not. My dad never worked and always claimed he was too sick; however, I knew he was nothing more than an angry, crazy drunk.

CHAPTER 3
A DAY OF BEING PENTECOSTAL

Finally, we were off that Sunday morning, traveling down the long, winding road that entwined itself around the skirts of the rolling hills. The only part I liked about attending church was the ride in the pickup truck and the endless rolling hills. I always loved seeing the church sitting in the tall grassy valley, thinking someone should capture this image in a picture. The farmers who lived around those parts built the little white church. It gave the ladies a place to worship and a place for their social gatherings. We finally got to church after a pee stop alongside the road; it was the first time my aunt was ever late. We made a dash right for our place, and of course, it was the front row marked for the saints.

I sat down in my spot right under the preacher's face in hopes he was off that garlic crave. I was so close to him that when he jumped and screamed, the smell was strong enough to coat my tongue. He was a massive man of great wisdom, with an appetite not only for food but also for the consumption of God's holy word. The man preached like thunder, echoing throughout the valley without missing a parcel of land. The farmers would say, "There isn't a place you couldn't hear Big John preach once he got up on his wooden crate."

I could tell we were late that Sunday morning because the pastor's bee-bees of spit were already scattered and lying around me. This preacher was burning the sulfur on that fine Sunday morning; the folks at the back row must have gotten him all fired up. He spat out those bee-bees from a huge mouth while using God's holy word, trying to turn it into buckshot as it flew over my head. It was his way of caring for the sinners perched in the back and not going with the flow on how to be saved.

I sat on the rock-hard pew, knowing my circulation was not at my end. If I could not feel my clean cheeks squeak, I knew they had also fallen asleep. My aunt tugged on the strap of my overalls, waking my butt up. Then I realized. It was time for the best part of being at church.

Every Sunday, the ladies would bring a box lunch because the drive home was a good piece of road. I would sit on the lawn eating my lunch when my big ears would get even bigger. It was my aunt's fault for pulling the potatoes out of my ears. I could hear what the ladies were saying while eating their lunch. My aunt always sat beside me, for she never participated in gossip. My Aunt Betty had her kind of pride. Most folks had it rough, for the land was harsh, and they just had to make do.

All the church ladies would complain about the selected few who had it better than the rest. They would call their fortunes the works of the Devil, and if their children were too proper and clean, they too must have gotten possessed. My aunt could only take so much, for she felt it was wrong, and they might as well have been out drinking and living it up.

We returned to the church's main hall, and my aunt said today was the church workday. I asked her what that was. She explained to me that the ladies would work on a project to sell at the county fair to raise funds to repair the church, and afterward, we could have a potluck,

I asked my aunt, "What is a potluck?" She replied, "Ronnie, there will be a lot of food, and until then, you can play with the other children." I like food and was always thankful for anything that took the hunger away. However, I wouldn't say I enjoyed playing with the church kids because there was indeed something different about them. They were well-dressed, and even the boys wore ties. All I had on were overalls and some worn-out shoes. I once had a nice shirt I grew out of; it was the best. It was a cowboy shirt that gunslingers would proudly display.

I spent the last part of the day playing alone in the muddy creek past the church. There were many tadpoles, and I would feed them pieces of bread. I had stuffed my pockets at the potluck to feed my friends.

Finally, my aunt said it was time to go, and I got in the pickup and stepped on the starter button on the floor. My aunt was amazed at how wet and muddy I had gotten. She wrapped me in a warm blanket, for my aunt knew the heater couldn't keep up with the cold wind blowing through the rusty holes in that old Ford pickup.

On the ride back, I was thinking about the kids at church and how their lives differed from mine. I wished I could live and feel like I belonged, not like I was just someone's problem. I felt as though my life was headed in the wrong direction. There was this big empty spot in the middle of my chest, and I didn't know how to fix it.

CHAPTER 4

LIFE WITH THE VANHOURNS

On the ride back, I fell into a food coma. When I woke up the next day, I was in a strange bed, wearing a nightgown well above my knees. I looked out the window and saw my clothes hanging out to dry on a clothesline that stretched from tree to tree.

My aunt came into the room and told me I was staying with her and for me to go and wash up for breakfast. I asked my aunt if my mother knew I was staying here. My aunt looked at me and said, "I do not think she has a choice." I did what she asked and walked out, finding all five were sitting at the table just waiting for me. I sat down, and CJ said, "Let's pray."

Things were strange to me sitting at a table full of food while going commando, meaning things were a little breezy under the table, for all I had on was this short nightgown. Their children consisted of two girls named Colleen and Katie, along with a boy whom I called Cricket; however, his name was really Jimmy. I met them a few times when CJ would visit his dad at his ranch. Uncle Frank always considered his boy a clown because he would do things that no one would think were funny.

I wanted to get dressed, but my clothes were still hanging on the clothesline, so I just sat in this strange place looking and soaking up the new surroundings. Everyone left to do their chores and left me inside the house to hang out until my clothes had dried. There was a big bang, and I knew it was a shotgun going off. I went out on the front porch and saw CJ holding a gun, pointing at the once-hanging clothesline. He yelled, "Rabbit squirrel, it was dashing down the clothesline, making fun of me!" I looked on the ground, and the only thing he killed was my underpants and overalls with that double-barrel shotgun.

My aunt was furious and demanded a word with this clown inside the house. Aunt finally came out of the house with Colleen, saying we were going into town to shop, and the rest of the kids were staying home.

I asked if they had something I could put on, and Colleen replied only if you like a prettier dress. That remark flew right over my head; I did not know what she was implying. Well, I asked, how about something I can tie around my waist? I could go looking like a Roman. They went into the house and came out with a blue ribbon so I could tie the nightgown down to keep it from flying up like an umbrella. Then I was happy and jumped into the back of the pickup while Aunt and Colleen rode in the front. We finally arrived and pulled into a spot down the street from the store. We all went in and walked by the store clerk, and he said, "If you ladies need help, just let me know." I did my best to keep my big mouth shut, for I noticed some church kids browsing for goods in the store.

Then, the proprietor who knew my aunt came over and asked who the new girl in town was. I quickly spoke up and said, "My name is Caroline, and it's nice to meet you, sir." The ladies held back, the best they could, from cracking up and laughing out loud at what I just said. Then I quickly spoke up again, saying we were shopping for my brother, who was the same size as me. The clerk was baffled because the only person not laughing were him and me. He said if you need help, ladies, you can ring the bell.

Well, we got the goods, and my aunt even bought me a pair of shoes, shirts, new overalls, a black tie, and underpants called whitey tidies. I jumped back into the pickup with my new goods after a late lunch at a café close to the store. I would have liked to have changed my clothes at the café; however, the place was crowded, and I was confused about what restroom to use. When we returned to the pickup parked down the street, I told my aunt, "You drive, and I will change my clothes in the back of the pickup."

I pulled off the nightgown and noticed that there were little blue bows located at the back. I looked up towards the pickup window, and there was Colleen with the biggest smile ever seen displayed by a girl. I could hear her yelling to her mother, "He just found out, and he looks like he may be a little ticked off." They did not know I had already figured It out by what the store clerk had said at the store.

We spent most of the day in town, and again, I was dirty after the ride home on the old dusty road. After a large dinner, a dinner that was fit for a king, it was time for bed. We were all lined up facing the large tin tub of water to receive our baths. The smallest one first and the biggest the last. I was third, and Colleen was behind me. I said we did not buy any nightgowns, and I was not wearing a dress. Colleen said. "Do not be alarmed. My mom removed the bows from the dress, and now it is just a nightgown."

The next day, Colleen had her twelfth birthday, and she had a cake with lovely white candles. I thought this was amazing as we sang, "Happy Birthday." Colleen was then presented with a birthday present. One time I went to my dad and said, "Today is my birthday," and Dad replied to me saying, "It's just another goddamn day." That was the only time I ever brought this subject up when I was supposed to have that special day.

Days and weeks went by as we worked, ate, and prayed. Things at church did not get any better because I still did not fit in with the children who played after church, even though I wore nice clothes. You know that old saying: if you put lipstick on a pig, it is still a pig. It was my troubled inner sole that was tainted by the hillbilly life from which I was hijacked from. I remembered a church song called "There is Trouble Within My Soul," which fit.

We worked and played hard with many opportunities to go skinny dipping at the swimming hole. These kids had no modesty at all, running around naked during parts of the day, not just at the swimming hole. They would sometimes take off into the fields or lay in the hay. Once, we ended up in the barn, and Colleen was lying next to me, staring at me, looking into my eyes as though she wanted to give me a lesson about "The Birds and the Bees." I admit she was beautiful with her long, straight blonde hair and stunning blue eyes; however, I had a good thing going and didn't wish to jeopardize being kicked out of this family. It was the first time in my life that I felt like I had a place where I belonged.

I would play with Jimmy in the shallow waters because I did not know how to swim. The girls played on the swing, dropping themselves off into the clear, deep waters. After weeks of living a free lifestyle, running around in the buff felt natural and not such a big deal.

One day at the swimming hole, Colleen told me, you do not have to jump off the swing into the water. You can swing across the pond and back by hanging on the rope. She said, "I will help you." Then she pushed off, and she went with me, wrapping her legs around my waist as we went out. Just then, the rope broke, and we went in. I panicked as she yelled, "Do not worry, I will save you." She grabbed me and instructed me to float on my back while I was pulled to the bank. It was like a fairy tale of being saved by a beautiful mermaid; however, one does not think this when you are drowning and sucking up a lot of water. We laid there on our backs, and I was coughing, and she asked if I needed mouth-to-mouth resuscitation. I said, "I don't know, what is that?" She said, "I will show you." Then she hovered over me and started blowing in my mouth, and then it turned into some strange kissing. I wouldn't say I liked it at first, but maybe it was all right.

Colleen smiled and giggled, saying, "I should be blowing up your lungs, but I think I may have accidentally blown up your binkie."

I was embarrassed because this had never happened, so I flipped over on my stomach, causing great pain to myself. I was trying to calm down because my heart was still pounding, and I was trying to catch my breath. Then she says, "You know you do not have to be like your father, and I do not see why others say terrible things about you."

That was enough to spoil my moment by bringing him back into my life. I asked, "What do others say about me?"

Colleen said, "I should not repeat it, for it is just rumors that are mostly untrue. I was told you are not his boy, and you do not even look like him." I said, "I know he must be because my mom says he is, and I never knew my mother to be a fibber."

I got up and got my clothes to go back to the house. I left her lying in the sun, for she was still a little cold from the swim.

In the evenings, there was always something to do, like play checkers and word games, and my aunt would always read to us; I remember winning the Good-do-Bee contest in the back of a children's book. I remember seeing a black and yellow bumble bee with a beautiful smile at the back. Since I won the contest, I wondered what I was supposed to get. CJ told me I won by showing things he never expected out of me, so he was going to take me out to target practice using a handgun. Most people I know said he was a clown; however, in my eyes, the whole family was clowns, and I will never forget the trip to town dressed as a girl.

School was in session, and I had some unlucky situations that would be filed in my memory for life. One day after school, I was held for detention, which happened, though not too often, because sometimes inappropriate words would pop out of my mouth. I headed home by myself, and it was raining heavily, and I was drenched down to my white. The lightning was bigger than the Mississippi River as it struck the ground. I did the only thing I could remember while in this situation. I got under a big tree and put my feet close together, hoping this storm would blow away. I woke up lying on a strange bed with a clean, dry pair of whitey tidies. It seemed like I was in a dream, finding my aunt washing my chest while ending the cleaning down below my belly button. I looked around and noticed everyone was there, looking and staring at me like they had seen a ghost. They said the tree was hit by lightning, and they had to drag me out. CJ said I was lucky this time, and there seemed to be no broken bones. However, your brain may have gotten a little fried, which is no joke.

Suddenly, the atmosphere was absent of any sound. It was like the sound was being sucked out in a vacuum. Just then, the wooden framed windows of the bedroom slammed wildly up, followed by a loud rumbling sound that shook the entire house. Then the house started shaking like a wet dog. The noise was incredible: it sounded like a freight train was passing by, and then there was silence. It was indeed Satan looking for some unsaved souls.

My aunt grabbed me, and they ran to the storage room because there was no time to make their way to the cellar. My aunt and the girls were praying heavily, and I was just like a blob, so weak I could not care less about what happened next. CJ went out of the room to look around, and after a few minutes, he returned, saying the coast was clear. They stuffed me back in bed, and I hoped that this was just one bad dream when I woke back up.

Later, we all found out that a tornado had developed right over our house, and the low pressure in the center of the storm sucked everything up and out. A weather forecaster in town said the house would have been blown apart if those old wooden windows had not opened so fast. It was also in the news that day that this twister hit the food store in town, killing two mothers and three children.

School was closing, and my mother sent word that she would pick me up on their way to California. I was not happy about it because why would I want to go back to living with a crazy drunk?

My aunt taught me a bedtime prayer, and I had to recite it whenever I went to bed. At the same time, she would pray for me in silence. Then my aunt would stuff me into bed and say she prayed that angels would watch over me.

Before I left, she gave me a copy of the bedtime prayer, "Now I lay me down to sleep, and I pray the Lord my soul to keep. If I die before I wake, I pray to the Lord my soul to keep."

She gave me a tablet with the Ten Commandments and the fifth one I had trouble understanding. You know, the one that says, "Honor thy father and mother." How do you honor a drunk who would beat you and your mother?

CHAPTER 5

ROAD TO CALIFORNIA

On a Sunday afternoon, when we returned from church, I saw my dad and mother sitting out in front of the house. CJ had my clothes already packed in a suitcase, and Colleen had my duffel bag with my prized belongings. Mom thanked Aunt Betty for watching me and instructed me to put my things in the car's back seat. The car trunk was already low to the ground, for I knew my dad was not going to California empty-handed. CJ asked my dad, who was sitting in the car, "You are not serious about taking that shine out of state." My dad just mumbled off a few swear words and then told me to get my ass into the back of the car. I could see my dad's eyes were bloodshot, and he was now looking pissed. I quickly removed the tie so that if we got into a fight, he could not use it to strangle me. As I got into the car, he reached over the car seat, giving me a welcome back knuckle sandwich, saying, "Don't touch my seat, you little shit!" I did not make a scene because people I cared about watched me as we said our goodbyes.

As we started traveling down the road, I checked to see why my duffle bag was so heavy. I looked, and I found that Colleen must have put a loaded handgun in my bag, and it was the one I was using for target practice. You could not believe the thoughts that went through my head. I always believe in a fair fight, and shooting someone in the back would be out of the question. I thought hard about that one. However, he was driving the car, and when it came to the fifth commandment, he was lucky, for I still had not figured out if this drunk was my father. Well, I thought that self-defense would work and could be an option. I fell asleep on my side of the car while feeling the pain in my head and not thinking of much. My sister was on the other side of the car and always just sat there, not saying a word. If we were talking to each other, I would always wind up getting smacked, and then my dad would call me a "God-damn-knucklehead." It is strange having a sister so close and yet so far away.

As I fell asleep, the dreams were many, and my soul was disturbed, for I left a family that cared about me. It did not take long for the dream I feared the most to latch onto my brain. I dreamed it a few times before, and if you dream something more than once, you begin to believe it happened. It is hard to forget your greatest fears, like the tornados and the person you feared most of all. But the one dream I feared had nothing to do with a person but a duel between Satan and me. How can you strike back at something you cannot see and do not know where to run from? I dreamed that I had gone to bed in an old dark storeroom which was lit up during the night by the harvest moon. The mattress stretched out on the wooden floor made up of various sizes and shapes of wooden planks. This storeroom had an old, broken-down door, which let in some moonlight, transforming it into ungodly illusions that danced for me around this dusty, dark room. I felt that others were present in this clammy cold room, for they were hiding in the shadows so that I couldn't see who.

I felt weary and alarmed, like that feeling you get when you think someone is watching you, but you do not know who. All at once, the wind stopped blowing, the crickets stopped singing, and the owl stopped hooting. I dreamed that night that Satan came to proclaim I was his. He said, "There is nothing you can do. You cannot see or touch me, and there is no place for you to hide. Your sole is mine."

I woke up sweating in the car's back seat and noticed that my mother was now driving. I asked what happened to Dad.? Mom said the cops got him with the goods in the trunk last night. Then she asked me why there was a loaded gun in my bag. I said, "Mom! I won it in a contest, and it's mine!" Mom said she gave it away to the cops, and they were not happy that a kid had a loaded gun. Mom said, "Ronald, you could have accidentally shot someone in this car."

I had now lost that opportunity. You know accidents do happen.

Everyone would always call me Ronnie. However, my real name given to me was Ronald, and it was only used when my mother was upset with me. Mother said she gave that name to me because she admired the actor named Ronald Reagan. I thought what she said hinted that my dad was not my father. If he were my father, why would Mother name me after some movie star she had a crush on? I was still thinking about the dream I had that night. I may have a few angels in my life; however, I only need to worry about one demon, and that would be the one that may take ownership of my soul.

I shook that dream off for another day and put on my happy face. Dad was gone, so I would enjoy my trip to California by taking in some roadside scenery of this vast desert land.

At the end of the day, we were driving by some honest-to-God- real-life Indians. They lined the roadside in great numbers; there must have been at least seven or eight. The teepee's bases were stretched out in their place in a vast circle so it could spin open to the top. The teepees were like a symbol that sat in their meant-to-be-places, holding up high values of what it takes to be noble. There were colorful printed patterns lined the bottom of these roadside temples, which were mysterious and brought character and charm to this vast, open land. Above the circular patterns running around the middle of the teepee were hand-painted figures of animals. My mother knew I was fascinated by the roadside Indians, so she told me about my dad and where he grew up. She said he went to school with the Indians in a place called the Cherokee Nation. It was a place where the United States government placed half a dozen tribes after forcing them off their land.

My mother said that grandma, who we were going to see, was a full-blooded Indian, so that would make Dad half-Indian.

I never knew my mom to be a fibber; however, I could tell when she was stretching the truth. I said, "Mom, if you put some feathers on Dad's head, he would look like an Indian I once saw called Sitting Bull. However, Mom, that name was taken so that I would have to call Dad Sitting Bullshit." My mom pulled over alongside the road. I said, "None of us in the back need to pee. Why are you stopping?" I knew why I was just trying to make conversation. She opened my door and told me to open it wide, referring to my big mouth, and then she stuffed a bar of soap in it. My mom said I had a potty mouth, and she was going to clean it up someday. I remember one time she stuffed a bar of soap in my mouth when I was mad. I thought I was going to piss her off and ate it as she watched me. That was a bad mistake on my part as I started vomiting my guts out as my mom called me a dumb ass. Later that day, if you think it is impossible to fart bubbles let me tell you that you are wrong. I was miraculously cleaning my underwear to the sound of every pop.

Back on the road again to California, and after some time had passed, my mother said, "We are now in the Golden State." I was amazed at how large the roads were. They even had bushes growing in the middle of the lanes. We only stopped a few times to stretch our legs and make a sandwich from the groceries in the car. We stopped a few times for gas so the gas-pumping man could fill our tank, check our oil, and give us some green chip stamps. That was nice; my pile of stickers was adding up.

After driving most of the day, we finally pulled off the road and headed down the streets looking for Grandma's house. I was disappointed to see houses lined up with such small yards. It was like looking at a line of chicken coops with little or no front porch. I wondered why anyone would give up their country life and move to live like farm animals.

CHAPTER 6

CALIFORNIA AVENUE

We finally parked in front of grandmother's house and walked through a small yard with a white picket fence looking no bigger than a pig pin. My grandmother moved out to California after my grandfather died. Grandma sold the Shell gas station located on Rute 66 in Oklahoma to buy this house for her retirement. I was told that for many years, she once played the piano for an Assembly of God church located right across the street from Richmond High School. Grandma was born in 1898 in or around the Cherokee Nation, and during her early life, there was no such thing as hopping in an automobile to go places. I was told she was a rugged woman and lived by her beliefs. One of her rules was that there was no such thing as credit or someone saying, "Just put it on my tab." Grandmother brought her family through the greatest depression ever known to happen in the United States. There was no such thing as welfare or food stamps. Many had to resort to soup lines to eat. Many of our relatives arrived in different states that did not want us, so I was told they gave us a nickname called Okies.

We got out of the car and walked to the little front porch. My sister and I just stood there as my mother went right in without knocking, and we followed her through the now-open door, hoping that this woman did not have a gun.

When we got in, we could see and hear my grandmother talking to my mother in a not-too-friendly way. Mom gave her the lowdown on what happened to Dad. Grandmother asked my mother if she had come to California to drop off another kid.

You see, no hospital was nearby if you lived in the sticks of Oklahoma. Mom always had complications with giving birth to her children. I was told when I was born, doctors had to separate me from my mother surgically. Mom would always come out to California for her medical needs, and then we would return to where we came from. This time, we all did not know that mom was not well, and it had nothing to do with dropping off another kid. We tried staying out of Grandma's way as we worked out in her little garden and even painted her shed. Grandmother would play some of her favorite church songs for us right before bed on her piano.

We were sleeping on the floor one fine morning, and I looked up. The crazy drunk was at my feet saying, "Get out of my way, you little shit." So, he went to the kitchen to have it out with his mother. You can see by looking into his eyes that he is not here for a social visit. I could hear him start in on Grandma by telling her all the wrong things she did in her life, especially when he came begging for help, and she did not act or act fast enough. He complained that when he asked for help at a time, the babies needed food, "Mom, you just let them starve." I did not know if he was referring to us or his first wife, who got away in the middle of the night. However, I was embarrassed by some of the things he said and how he carried on.

The biggest complaint he had with his mom was that she did not act fast enough to get him out of the United States Army's mental institution. The Army drugged him off the battlefield during the Second World War and deemed him to be crazy. The army's witch doctors put him in for medical treatment by giving him electrical shocks to the brain trying to fix his wagon. Grandmother had to sign my dad out of the government's nut ward and take full responsibility for him. This closed the door for any' assistance, financially, medically, or any responsibility that the United States government may have once had. Dad continued for more than an hour, and I knew we would not be welcome to stay another night at Grandma's house, so I started packing our things while my mother and my sister just sat in the front room listening to his crap.

Before Dad finished another cup of coffee, he told us to pack our things and get ready to go. I wanted to stay or get a bus ticket to go back to live with Aunt Betty. I was dreaming because I knew that was not going to happen. I started burning my brain cells thinking about why I needed to be with this family, for I was just another mouth to feed.

A few days before we left Grandma's house, she gave me two gifts. One was a piano book of songs she once played for the church she belonged to. The second gift was a United States Census report that showed the names and ages of her family members at the time of the report. The report taken in 1900 disclosed that Grandma was in Indian territory, which was the Cherokee Nation. Back in Grandma's days, there was no such thing as a birth certificate, and you had to rely on what the United States Census report disclosed. My grandmother told me she escaped from the Cherokee Nation by cutting off her pigtails and walking off. Grandma said most Indians registered with the Government to get a roll number. However, her family opted out. I asked her if she was Cherokee, and she said no. Grandma said she was from the Choctaw tribe, one of the seven tribes; however, the United States Government would only recognize six. I said that would make me a quarter Indian, and Grandma laughed loudly, "It depends on who your father is child."

I told her if that was supposed to be a joke I was not laughing.

Grandma said, "Kid, you don't have any facial traits of an Indian when I look at you. You have streaks of light blond hair throughout your hair, and I have never seen that in an Indian boy. Plus, you have this funny, cute foreign accent like you just stepped off a boat."

I said, "Grandma, you know my mom is Irish."

CHAPTER 7

HOME IS WHERE YOU MAKE IT

Dad drove us to a shop and bought a tent, fishing poles, and some other necessities, and then we traveled out of town to a riverbank named Knights Landing. To avoid the law so they would not take notice that we were living on the riverbanks, we moved to various locations. I really liked this fishing spot that was named Whiskey Slough. It has a lot of large trees, and the fish are biting. By then, Dad somehow obtained a frog boat so we could go out gigging for, you guessed it, frogs. We would peddle the boat down the river at night, and the frogs would bellow so loud you think they were calling for us, saying, "Come and get me." We would sneak up on them, and as I shine the light into their eyes, my dad would stab them with a sharp fork at the end of the pole. The pole looked like a miniature version of the devil's pitchfork that brought death to the poor soul at the other end. After getting our gunnysack full, we returned to camp to sleep the rest of the night away. The next day, Mom would fry the frog legs up on a campfire using an iron skillet, adding seasoning to turn it into a tasty dish.

After a few days passed, Dad built a dock for the frog boat by using old trees that had fallen to the ground on the sides of the river's bank. It was a nice boat dock, making this location a prideful spot. It brought envy to other fishermen as they would motorboat by our camp, asking if we caught anything.

We went into town to buy chicken guts to set out our droplines, hoping to catch some large catfish. We always caught whoppers, and I liked eating catfish because they did not have too many bones to avoid. The thing I didn't like was using my fingers to pinch the air out of these guts to be used for bait. Catfish were bottom feeders, and the best way to hook one was to ensure the food was lying on the bottom. Any air inside would cause the guts to float to the top. It was hard to get that chicken gut smell off my fingers, and when I ate a sandwich, it did not taste so good. I did not think at that time it was legal to set out so many droplines. Dad was not acting himself when sneaking around in the dark of the night to avoid detection. We hooked so many catfish that Dad would go into town and sell them to mom-and-pop grocery stores.

One morning, an officer of the law came into our camp, asking questions and looking around. Then the officer looked into my eyes, saying, "How many lines do you have out?" I turned my attention to my mother, and she looked like she would faint. I kept my big mouth closed for now. Dad was off the bottle, and there was no need at this time for me to rat on him. My mom kept staring at me as the law enforcement officer turned his questioning toward Dad as he came out of the tent. Mom looked frightened because she thought I would not keep my big mouth shut. Dad would just get in trouble, but she knew he would whip us both the next time he got drunk. Dad told the lawman a big fib so he would go away.

We did inherit a stray dog who found us on the banks of the river. It was small but quite clever. Mom named her Bunny, which I thought was odd for a dog. This dog became my best friend and kept me warm at night as I slept on the riverbanks. My sister enjoyed Bunny because sometimes she crawled between us.

My sister and mom would do their thing most of the time, and I was just like a baseball player sitting on the bench.

After a few months of this outdoor living, my mom said we needed to find a place to live. She said we should move closer to town so she could find a job. The money paid to my dad from Uncle Franks's employment will soon run out. I loved living on the banks of the river, and my mom really kept a clean tent.

We moved in with my dad's brother, known to me as Uncle Tommy, and his wife, Aunt Peggie. My mother was now pregnant again and had someone to watch us kids.

This new one, James Jobe, came along, for he was named after my dad's grandfather. I was unhappy about this situation; for now, I had someone else I must avoid to keep from getting smacked. Aunt Peggie stayed with the newborn while Mom went to work as a waitress so we could get our own place. Dad did get hammered a few times; however, his brother was too forgiving.

CHAPTER 8

TWENTY-FIRST STREET

When we moved to our new place, my sister was a tremendous help in caring for the little kid we nicknamed Joey. Throughout our grammar school years, we found ourselves mostly unsupervised and had to care for our needs. Most of the time, we would leave the door open even if no one was home. Sometimes, you may have a neighborhood kid snooping around. However, no one was looking for trouble.

The restaurant Mom worked at was open twenty-four hours a day, and she did her best to work at night to make time to be with her children. Mom often worked double shifts and would usually be at home but asleep.

We moved into an old shack rented by a Mexican family that would be living next door. This old house had a little kitchen sink that once belonged to a camping trailer, so there was little room to wash the dishes. The driveway was nothing more than rocks and weeds, making it the saddest-looking house in the neighborhood. The only thing that kept this house from falling apart, I was told, was that they found that the termites were holding hands. It was a one-bedroom house, and with three kids, it would indicate that Mom and Dad would be sleeping on the couch. This old house was a few houses from the creek, which, to me, became my highway to get around town. My school was only one long block away and had a fancy name: Dover Elementary. One day after school, I cut my name on the sidewalk at school. I did it after the city's maintenance people poured the cement, and I found it was still a little wet by the time I arrived. Walking west into the creek, I could get to the nice big park called Davis Park. I played a lot in this park because they had a park assistant named Ms. Boots who would let you check out some games.

This city also had several creeks that kids used to get around town. It was like a highway for children to come and go. I was also within walking distance of a Sunny Side Market grocery store, where I would buy mom or dad a pack of cigarettes or whatever they requested. Most of Dad's family lived in this town, which was also my grandmother's hometown.

The only dreadful thing about this location is that it had twenty-three bars for my dad to hide out in. At times, when Mom needed him home to watch Joey, she had to hunt him down by calling all the bars. This made him turn into a monster, for when he got home, he would slap mom around the house, saying, "God damn you woman! 'Don't you ever come looking for me woman!"

As a new fourth-grade student, I found that many children attending this school were like me. They were children brought here because their parents were looking for a better life, and if it did not happen, there was welfare to fall back on. My mother avoided the welfare office because they asked too many questions. Mom was always trying to keep the family together, for that was the only thing she had in her life, and she did not need the law to come snooping around.

Mom went as far as making sure my sister never attended the same school I did. Mom did not need my sister to give Dad a report on me when I got home from school. She knew he would physically harm me if my sister said the wrong thing to him. When Dad was pissed off at me and even when he was not on the bottle, he would kick me with his foot, swearing and telling me to stay away from her.

My mom always made sure there was food at home for us to prepare so we would not go hungry. We had TV dinners and pot pies to put in the oven. I knew how to make breakfast; Mom even taught me to make gravy from scratch. It took me a few tries, but I learned the science behind it. Mom said you would never go hungry if you knew how to make gravy.

Often, I would make dinner or breakfast for my sister, and her job was to feed the little kid when needed. I also would feed our dog daily with a half can of dog food called Skippy. If I needed anything, I always got the money to buy it, as I would collect Coke bottles, and at that time, it was worth a lot for recycling. I would rent our lawn mower out to the neighbors who needed one. My best money came from cleaning or sweeping bars and store parking lots.

Often, Dad would be at the bar drinking it up, and I would run around town doing my thing. One day, a man of God came to me and asked if I would like to go to church on Wednesday nights after school, and for some reason, I said yes. His name was Brother Strong, and he would pick up street children and take them to his church in the hope of saving their souls. He cleared it with Mom, and my sister did go a few times, but that was all. When there was an altar call, Brother Strong would push us kids to the altar to pray for our needs. We were a squad of dirty children with rugged clothes, and after a few months, we wore out our welcome. Finally, the Assembly of God church pastor came to speak with Brother Strong as I stood beside them. He told Brother Strong that we were too dirty and were disrupting his congregation. The pastor agreed that having one or two children on Wednesday night would be appropriate, but not half a dozen.

After church service or what was left of it, Brother Strong would take us to Froster Freese to get a cup of ice cream. That was our reward for being good in church. After that night, Brother Strong would take us to a different church every Wednesday, hoping we would not wear out our welcome. He would study what the preacher was saying and sometimes herd us out by pushing us into a single file, saying this is a bad church.

On altar calls, I would kneel in an open spot until I thought it was time to return to my seat. I didn't know how to pray or ask God for anything. And if I did ask God for anything, would I know if he hears my cry for help? I was just a kid. Still, there was no lack of church members placing their hands on me and praying for me. I remember telling Jesus 'If you would like my soul, it is yours." It was a time when no one hugged me or even showed concern for me. I would not have understood your question if you had asked me about love. I never knew what that was.

Life was rough with a father who was always angry with me, and he never said anything to me unless it was an order to do something or he just wished to swear at me for something I did or did not do.

I thought I'd try something different and start praying to Jesus's Mother because I thought she would be less busy and more caring. I asked her if she could protect me and send angels per my Aunt Bette's request. I am not afraid of man, just the demon they had let into their souls. One evening, the group leader played a game, and I won a picture of Jesus, which I proudly placed on the wall at the foot of my bed.

A week or so had passed when another Christian man came to the door and asked Mom if I would like to join the Boys Scouts of America. I was excited until he told my mother it was not free and would cost her a few dollars. She was hanging on by a thread, trying to pay rent and feed an alcoholic. She politely said no. I was devastated and just went to cry in silence, turning my anger to God because we were so poor.

I tried to stay out of Dad's way. However, he spent a lot of time in bars and tinkering with things like building frog boats, fishing, or playing with the animals he kept in the backyard. Our backyard looked like a farmhouse, with chickens, ducks, and rabbits. When my dad demanded my help, I went with him and did whatever he said. I was always afraid if I did not do the job right, he would hit or kick me.

Once, he got a side job tearing down a building for some cash on the side, and I had to go with him. I was sick and not much use to him and went and laid down in the pickup. I was there for hours, and the only thing to drink was this large bottle of wine sitting on the floorboard of the pickup. I got so drunk I had to crawl outside for some fresh air. I remember leaning with my back against the fender of the pickup, dropping my shorts while Binky was attempting to spell my name on the sidewalk. Then I got back in and drank some more of the juice until I passed out. Then I remember Dad pulling into our driveway as a little breeze touched my back. The windows were down, and Mom was coming back from work. I was lying on the seat of the pickup when I heard Mom ask, "Where is Ronnie?" I heard Dad replying, saying to Mom that I was in the pickup truck drunk. I was so drunk I could not move or even open my eyes, so I just blacked out. I woke up in the middle of the night still lying on the black leather seat of the pickup and was in disbelief that they had left me outside in the driveway. I pulled off my first drunk and was not even out of the fourth grade.

I went to school sick in the morning, and when the teacher asked me what was wrong, I told her I had a hangover. The teacher did not believe me. Who would even think a kid at that age would show up at school with a hangover?

I ran around town and played in the park, and sometimes Bunny would go with me. That dog would protect me if another kid raised their hand to me in anger; however, she knew better when it came to the drunk of the house to stand back. One time Bunny tried to step in to protect me from the wrath of Dad's anger, and he kicked the crap out of her as well.

I was never good in school; however, I did try my best, considering the circumstances I had to deal with. I remember I would study all weekend for a spelling test and go to school thinking I was going to get one 100 percent correct, and instead, I was one 100 percent wrong. I was disturbed by why I couldn't spell anything right, and there was no shortage of red ink. I liked going to the library next to our school to look at the pictures because I couldn't read, and when I tried, it felt like my brain would fall out of my head. I would get unbelievable headaches to the point where I had to lie down with my eyes closed, hoping the throbbing pain in my head would go away.

Mom spent some time at home healing after the operation. She had a tumor in her stomach removed, and Christmas was now approaching. We never expected much, and if we did get something for Christmas, it was bought at a secondhand store. It was Christmas Eve, and there was nothing under our tree. However, we did have a tree.

Then came a knock at the door, and when Mom opened it, some of Mom's coworkers were bringing gifts for all to enjoy. My sister and I were blessed that year with new bikes, and mine was a three-speed. It only took a week for someone to steal my sister's bike because she would never put it away. I needed to protect my property, so I went to the police department and paid a dollar for them to hammer out an identification number onto the bottom of my frame. Along with that, the officer put a sticker displaying the year.

I left the police department, and within a few blocks away, I was walking across the crosswalk, looking down at my nice white reflective sticker. The next thing I remember, I thought I was in a dream looking up at the bottom of a car motor while it was still running. The driver didn't see me when he turned the corner because he was too busy talking to someone in the passenger seat. When I woke up, I was lying on a table looking at a man dressed in a white gown, and this funny-looking contraption pointed at my head. I was naked, and he said, "We are going to take X-rays to see if anything was broken." He then taped some shield over Binky, and wouldn't you know it, Binky refused to stay down, and I was a little embarrassed. He didn't say anything and used a lot more tape. Afterward, I was wheeled into a room with Mom, and we waited maybe a half hour or so. Then, a doctor walked in with his chart, saying, "Boy, you must have had an angel looking over you because you were just knocked out by the car." Mom said the policeman came running down the street, the one that stickered my bike, and ordered a lot of men to pick the car up off me for I was wedged under it with my crumpled-up bike.

Well, like all poor people, Mom took the driver to court. However, the judge put a small amount of money into a trust fund for me until I turned eighteen but also provided funds to cover a new bike. Mom was upset because she paid for this ambulance chaser and got nothing in return. I never got a new bike; the money went into Mom's pocket.

Dad was back to his uncontrollable drinking and would get into fights at the bar and then come home running like a bloody coward. One time, he woke up the following day needing a drink and demanded money from Mom. Mom said the wrong thing by claiming she was penniless, and during Dad's search, he found the rent money, and crap was now going to hit the fan. He grabbed her by the hair and slammed her up against the wall, saying, "Damn you, woman, don't you ever hide money from me!" Dad left with the cash and went off drinking the night away.

Dad would return home after the bar closed, always around 3 am, and he would come looking for me. He would grab me out of bed and slam me against the sofa. Mom was already on the floor from the not-so-friendly greeting he gave her when she opened the door. Same old story, same old crap about how he came home and found mom somehow had gotten pregnant. Dad would go at me with unbelievable anger as this nut job preached to me that I'm not his son and never will be. I would sit there wishing I had a gun so I could take care of this psycho's problem he had with me. Dad would curse at me in anger and hate. He knew how to push the wrong buttons; however, he always stopped short of calling my mother a whore.

Mom must have gone to work the following day, and Dad was in the kitchen with my sister. I said I was hungry and would like something to eat, and he kicked me so hard I was launched into the other room. I was in shock; he finally caught me off guard. With no place to run, I ran to school until it was time to take my seat. The teacher noticed I was in pain and bleeding from my chest. I was ordered to go to the principal's office, and so I did. I was dirty, with one button left on my shirt, and my skin was scraped from my chest. The principal came over as I sat in his office crying, and he kneeled over and asked me if my father had done this. I nodded to him in a yes gesture, for I felt ashamed. The authorities came to my house to question my parents and informed them if it happened again, the boy would be taken and placed into a foster home.

I don't know if anyone had to go to court over this; however, it gave my dad a new weapon. My dad would threaten me, saying If I didn't do what I was told, he was going to give me away to the county.

I hated this government, for they made my life a living hell. This government released a mentally ill nut job on me and my mother and then gave him a tool to make me his slave. If the Army had kept him, I still might have been born, for remember, the drunk keeps telling me I'm not his.

From that day on, when we said the pledge of allegiance to the flag at school, I placed my hand over the permanent lump that Dad put on my chest by breaking my rib. It was the rib right over my usually empty stomach. I was confused about how the United States government could do this to a kid. And at times, when we pledge our allegiance to the flag, a tear would fall to my pink cheek. The teacher must have thought this boy must be very patriotic; however, I thought Dad won for now. Yes, now two people in this family were mentally disturbed. I also swore I would never put my hand over my heart and pledge any allegiance to this country again.

I was also angry at Jesus, who was hanging at the end of my bed, and I turned this picture into nothing more than a giant dartboard. As I slung darts at him, I would shout. Words of unwisdom, and did I know many. This went on for a few weeks until nothing was left of him.

Then, another evening, when I went to church with Brother Strong, I started crying at the altar; I felt my life had no purpose. I couldn't stop crying. With my eyes closed, all I see is darkness, no lights of hope; no one is coming to rescue me. No one wants me, and I'm going to be alone forever. I was catching my tears with the palms of my hands as I fell sideways on the carpet, crying in a fetal position. I felt this massive hole in the middle of my chest and didn't know how to fill it. Many church elders came and placed their hands on me, praying for me. After a while, Brother Strong realized I wasn't going to stop crying, so he carried me back into his van and went for the other children. You know after a good crying, sometimes life seems to be a little better and not all as bad as one would think.

Some weeks passed, and then I came down with chicken pox, missing school for over a week. My brave teacher walked from school to our house with a lot of schoolwork. I don't know if she was interested in my education, or maybe she thought Dad had buried me in the backyard. She walked up to the front door, which was open except for the screen door. Dad saw her coming and opened the screen door as I stood there and watched. My teacher handed the schoolwork to my dad, saying she was concerned about me falling behind. My dad took the papers from her and launched them over her head and all over the yard, saying in extreme anger, "God-Dammit! when he is here, he is here to work, and when he is at school, he is there to learn." I watched my teacher run out through the picket-fenced yard, and all I remember was seeing the bottom of her black high-heeled shoes as she frantically ran back down the sidewalk. My mouth dropped wide open, and I thought my life was indeed ruined. I had no more dignity, no reason to go back to school. I knew if this teacher hadn't seen me, she would have called the authorities.

Dad found other ways to torture me besides turning me into his slave. He called me to the backyard and had my sister's pet chicken named Ruby. Then, as he made me watch him, he ripped off her head, laughing at me, as it ran around headless in the yard until she dropped dead. I looked at him with unbelievable hate for this person, which quickly turned into fear as I ran back into the house.

He also brought me out to San Pablo Bay, and the waves of water were so bad they were going over the sides of this little frog boat. He wanted to go out to the duck blinds and told me to get in. I wondered why he had no shotgun or fishing pole, and we both knew I couldn't swim. I looked at him and said, 'That's not going to happen." Dad said, "What did you say to me, you little shit!" I said, "You are trying to drown me, aren't you?" Dad gave me an evil smile and told me to get my little ass back into the pickup.

Another time, Dad was drunk and pushed me into his pickup for a ride. He drove me to the top of the place called Tank Farm Hill, and as we went back down, it was at an incredible rate of speed. Dad's eyes were not on the road. He was staring at me with uncontrollable laughter. I could honestly see this person was insane, and he would repeatably yell at me, "Are you scared!" Damn right, I was frightened so bad I was stiff as a wooden plank. He enjoyed seeing me frightened, or was he making sure I was so scared of him I would never talk to the law?

I had a brown teddy bear I would sleep with until my teddy went missing one night. I knew that the ass of the house kidnaped Teddy. Well, what the hell, I thought. Maybe I'm too old to sleep with a teddy bear.

Things were cooling off, or maybe my dad had run out of ways to mess with my head.

The landlord grew tired of Dad and told Mom we would have to find another place to live by the next school year.

Many neighborhood boys needed something, maybe a word called supervision. Once, I walked into a friend's house a few houses down from me and found six boys playing strip poker. The largest item was first, and the smallest was last, and there were already two boys down to just one or two socks. They asked me to join, and I had to ante up my pants to get into the game. I said no because I knew I would lose, and standing there naked sounded stupid to me.

A few weeks later, I followed the same group of boys into a meat packing plant as they broke in from under the floor. They started destroying the place and all the equipment when they got in. I was frantically trying to stop them and found it was hopeless. I was so frightened I couldn't breathe, so I high-tailed it out of there. Each boy's parents had to pay for the damages which was in the thousands of dollars. The cops left me out of this because two of the boys told the authorities that I was trying to stop them, but there were too many of them and just one of me.

The kids on the block unfriended me because they felt my mom should have helped pay for the damages. After all, I was there with them. I didn't need any additional problems, so I avoided them.

With the lack of friends, I sometimes wander up and down the creeks alone. I would also walk through cemeteries reading gravestones. The cemeteries were quiet, and I believed I could talk to Jesus's mother; I thought I could feel her presence. I felt as if she was there listening as I revealed my troubles. Sometimes, I would cry a little because my troubles were deep. It was a quiet place, and I was there looking for answers. At times, I would come across the young and wonder if my life would be cut so short. There were children like me, and some of the gravestones would have pictures of who was occupying the little plot of land. I attended a funeral service once, and everyone looked and stared at each other, wondering to whom this kid belonged. However, no one said anything until I ran off after the pastor said, "Amen.

I often played at the park alone, and when I was home, I did anything I was commanded to do. I sometimes grew tired of the slave work and hated this thing called the ironing board.

I would watch television indoors if Dad were nowhere to be found. When my dad was home, I confined myself to what I felt was a safe place: my bed. My bed was known to me as a place where I couldn't get in trouble. It was not all that safe, for I sometimes heard footsteps walking on the sidewalk at night. This went on for months, and it frightened me to where I would stay awake all night. I thought it was Satan coming to claim me, for no one else wanted me. One night, when awakened by footsteps, I realized where the sound was coming from. The beating of my heart sounded like footsteps against the sidewalk. This sidewalk was right outside my bedroom window. I was relieved it wasn't someone or some creature looking to harm me.

I wish I had parents who could comfort me if I were frightened. Someone I could go to if someone harmed me. Someone I could talk to about my deepest secrets, like, for example, if some pervert had his way with me. I know if I said anything, my dad would just beat the crap out of me or send me off to the county. It was always my fault, no matter what the circumstances were. It was best to keep my mouth shut when something bad happened.

\

CHAPTER 9

UNIVERSITY AVENUE

Another school year had come, and we moved to this other substandard house built during the war. However, it was larger than the shack we were kicked out of. It had a big yard, two bedrooms, and an attached shed, which I called my room. A creek was across the street, and the post office was at the other end of the block. Adjacent to this post office was a bar with a little convenience store attached to it. I was still within walking distance of Sunny Side Market, so that did not change; however, I will now attend a school called Broadway Elementary. One lady owned this whole block of homes that she rented out. Oddly, my mother was the only person working on this street. The rest were single mothers with children drawing welfare checks and food stamps.

Finally, we settled into our new place, and I was surprised; the girls in this neighborhood outnumbered the boys six to one. I was a follower, not a leader, and felt powerless regarding a girl's will. One time, Debbie, my neighbor next door, snuck into our house, and I could see her walking towards me as I peeked out of the crack of my eye. I was lying on my couch pretending to be asleep with my mouth a little open as she gave me a long, passionate kiss. I just laid there, pretending to be a heavy sleeper, not to embarrass her. Then, as she slid her tongue to my ear, she whispered, saying, "I know you're awake," as she ran out the door. I must omit that she made my day, and I think I could not get my mind off that for over a month. I think I was the most groped-on boy in the neighborhood. There were some incredible stories about the girls on University Avenue, and I will never forget the fun those naughty girls had with me. One girl dragged me into a shed, one under the camper shell, and another insisted we try out her new bottle of bubble bath. I was eleven and a half years old, harmless, but unknowingly, puberty was just around the corner. The girls in this neighborhood insisted on expanding their education.

My mother once took me to her friend's house, which had a daughter a few years older than me. My mom and her friend went into the backyard and left me alone in the house with this big, weird girl. It was stupid of me to walk with her into her bedroom. She picked me up and threw me on her bed; she mounted me as if I were a horse and then flipped herself around for some backward saddle riding. I tried fighting back on this unexpected maneuver, for she was not even close to being a beauty queen. We both stayed as quiet as a mouse; it would have been horrible if our parents walked in on this. I lost the fight and was amazed at how she overpowered me as if I were a ragdoll. She stripped me from the waist down by hanging me upside down and dropping my nuts out of my shorts like a sack of potatoes. She threw me back down for some more saddle riding. I found her hands to be icy cold when she grabbed me. She popped her dress up, putting her butt in my face, smothering me. Then she dropped her panties to give me a good look and started rubbing her behind in my face. I put my teeth into her bare rump, making sure I went for the tender part so I could get a large bite. She squealed like a pig, saying," You hurt me!" She was furious as she flew off me, holding onto her butt. She went looking in the mirror to check out the bite as her panties dropped to her feet. I was terrified because I could hear my mom and her friend talking outside in the backyard. Yelling out for help would not have been wise, for girls can do as they wish. However, if a boy did what she did to me, they would be sent to the big house. It was always the boy that got the shaft and was the predator. I quickly got dressed, went outside to sit in the car, and waited for Mom.

I didn't know why we were at this stranger's house or why my mom and her friend were hiding out in the backyard. This girl's mom was the size of a bear, and her daughter was not much smaller. I did know that Mom's friend was all over the news. A car fell on her neighbor when it was sitting on blocks. The news proclaimed that this woman dashed out of her house with superhuman strength and picked the front of the vehicle off him, saving his life.

My mother finally came around the side of the house as this girl came out her front door. She lifted her dress enough to show my mom the bite I put on her butt. My mom's face turned red as she laughed; one could only think this was a setup. On the ride home, I told my mom I didn't like her and what you did was evil. My mom said she was looking for a babysitter so they could run off to Reno for a night out of town. I said that would never happen," I'm too young to be a father." Mom said, "She is harmless." Mom asked me why I bit her, and I said to Mom because she put her butt where it didn't belong.

Maybe I would have been better off playing with the boys than the girls in the neighborhood. However, the boys didn't like me, and I didn't care. There were plenty of girls to occupy my time with. So, I learned to play Jacks, Hopscotch, Red Light, Green Light, etcetera. When it came to doll playing, all the girls were older than me and well past the stage of playing with baby dolls.

Mom and dad did take off to Reno, however I went with them. They left me out in the car around two in the afternoon. I sat there until midnight, and to my surprise, they both came out and fell in the back seat of the car drunk. I had never seen my mother drunk in my life, so now what should I do? I was freezing and hungry, and we had no money for a place to stay, so I got the keys and drove them back up and over the mountains. The mountains must have been nine thousand feet above ground elevation. I had never driven a car before, and this one was a little foreign automobile with a stick shift. Almost four hours later, we finally made it back home. I parked and left the drunks in the back of the car, went into the house, and found the babysitter in my bed. I was exhausted and laid down between the wall and her with just my whitey tighties on. I told her if she did anything funny, I would bite her. She said it was her time of the month, whatever that meant. I told her I was too young to be a father, and she said don't worry, I am safe. I thought that was the same thing my mom said, so I asked her what it meant. She said she was on birth control to regulate her period. I went to sleep, a little confused about what she said. I woke up and found I was wearing her panties, and she made off with my undies. However, she left me a note saying thanks for the sleepover. I sleep like a rock and hope nothing happened that night; if it did, I would never remember it.

Two boys were Sergeant Fry's nephews who lived a few houses down from me and would always start fires in the creek to see the fire department put them out. I would fight them both simultaneously because they would call me an Okie. This happened a few times; however, I always won the fights. The law officer grew tired of coming out to rescue his boss's nephews. I noticed he had big ears as he was checking me out. The officer said, "One more time, boy, I'm taking you off to juvenile hall." Well, I thought it best to stay away from them. It's nice if your uncle is a cop and can protect you even if you're in the wrong.

I was upset when I found out that it was my mom who was calling the cops on me. I said to my mother, "Do it again, and I will call the cops on you when you get into a fight with Dad." She looked at me with a face filled with incredible anger, wishing to whip my little butt for saying that; however, I thought I was smart enough to have the phone in my hand. I was angry and felt betrayed. What mother would turn her son in to the police?

Mom went outside and came back in with an impressive-looking switch and said, "You little shit!" Then she started putting whip marks all over me. I didn't have a shirt on, and she delivered the pain for what I just did. She angrily said, "Not only you but your sister and brother would be taken away." I was in a lot of pain, lying on the floor crying, rubbing the bright red lashes mom had put on my body. Mom returned outside, got into her car, and left for work. I wished I could have run away from home, but there wasn't any place I could run to. I felt like Mom after she got her butt stomped by Dad. I thought, who would want me? I was in a trap. I felt that there was no escape.

During the last part of the summer before school started, Dad would go fishing on days Mom wasn't working. Mom was working, off and on, through my grammar school years because of her operations. I will never forget one day she came home crying because she said she had cancer. I was horrified at the thought of something happening to

Mom. Without a doubt, I would have a one-way ticket to the county.

I have only seen Mom cry two times in my life when it was not connected to a beating from Dad. Once, she came home from finding out she had cancer, and anyone could understand that. Then, the other time, I came home from school and found her crying at the kitchen table. I asked her, "Why are you crying?" Mom said, "I can't believe I owe taxes; we are so poor and have nothing." Well, I thought to myself, it takes a lot of money to feed three children and an out-of-control drunk.

The anger that Dad had for me calmed down at times because of Mom's illness, and he was like a crazy wild ape in a corner just waiting to start something. I was attending a new school and had hoped my dad would turn over a new leaf and stop physically harming me. I hoped this new school had no information about me and my dad.

Right before school started, I played down the street at another adjacent creek behind the newly installed John F Kennedy Memorial. I was on the bank side of the creek, and my friend that I was with noticed the ground would move when I walked on it. I thought I would impress him and started stomping on the ground with my feet. Then suddenly, a giant underground sinkhole opened and swallowed me. Halfway down this deep sinkhole, I was hanging onto the only tree root in this huge pit, which was the size of a swimming pool. The hole was deep and full of mud, and indeed, I would have been buried alive.

It was like an angel placed this tree root in my hands. My friend called out to me and said he would get help. He quickly brought two older boys back, and they were able to rescue me by using a long branch from a tree. I was very muddy and cold, so I walked to the plaza's fountain to wash myself off. I was freezing, and it felt warm when I jumped into the water. I walked home, but it was so cold; my little body was shivering. I went into my room, put on some clean underwear, crawled into bed, and tried to warm myself up.

When night came, I was coughing and gagging all night long. I was so sick, and it was later confirmed by the hospital that I did get water in both lungs, which quickly turned into pneumonia. I never told Mom what happened at the creek, and she would never believe me anyway; I don't believe it happened myself. Later, the Richmond Independent reported that the twenty-foot sinkhole was the fault of an underground gas line that had been leaking for years. I must have never stopped coughing for nine months and couldn't run or overexert myself.

I tried my best in the fifth grade and studied more than ever because I was too sick to play. One day, I stood out in the school's hallway, and my teacher told this fourth-grade teacher that this boy, who was me, couldn't even spell the street he lived on. At that time, no one knew I was dyslexic and not stupid; I couldn't spell anything that was more than two syllables.

I became an after-school traffic guard at that school, which made me feel needed. It felt a little strange to me, you know, to be needed. Right before the bell rang, I was allowed to go to the storage room and meet the other children from other classrooms. We would quickly put on our red uniforms and grab stop signs to use in the streets to stop traffic so other children could cross safely.

I was happy to have something nice and clean to put on because I was often dirty with a ragged shirt and holes at the bottom of my shoes. One morning, I was walking to school with the neighborhood children, and I vanished into a creek when they weren't looking. I was so dirty, with rags hanging off my body, and I was embarrassed. I went and hid in the creek crying, and undoubtedly, the school notified the cops. The cops found me as I was crawling out of my hiding place. I was at the side of the creek with tears dripping off my face, so I said I was just a little sick, so they took me to the school nurse. She looked me over, cleaned me up, and gave me a shirt from Lost and Found hanging in the closet from last year's school session.

Dad stayed away from me when I came home from school because I was ill, or maybe he was afraid of the law. He was on a new schedule for this year, which was just a bi-weekly drunk; however, he would now leave me out of his rage of anger. Dad just beat up Mom and, at times, destroyed some of the furniture before he passed out. One day after school, Mom packed everything in the car, including my brother and sister, then ordered me to get in. Mom had two enormous black eyes, and it frightened me. I asked her what had happened, and she said she ran into a lamp. Dad once again stomped the crap out of her, and she'd had enough; she was leaving.

As we drove off and down the road, it was the happiest day of my life. She drove around town for a few hours, and then we returned to our dirt-filled driveway. She put her head on the wheel and started crying again. We had done this a few times before, except now I was crying with her. We all went back into the house and dragged the drunk into the bedroom so we could clean up the house he had destroyed.

When we drove around town that day, I wondered, did my mom do this years ago and find herself in another man's arms? That would explain why my dad was not my father. I always wondered why Dad would stop short of calling my mom a whore. On many of his out-of-control drunken rages, he always made sure he told me I was not his. Maybe Mom found herself in a worse situation than the one she had left and came crawling back to him. Or maybe Dad was in jail, and when he came out of the slammer, Mom had somehow gotten pregnant.

Finally, school was out, and I was entering the sixth grade. My Uncle Elzey invited me to camp up north at his property all summer and look for gold. We traveled to a burned-out gold mining camp in the City of Washington, California. Mom let me go with him, even though he was also an alcoholic; however, he wasn't an angry one.

We searched the mountains and rivers for gold, and I understood why he needed me. I was his donkey, carrying all the equipment while he carried his bottle. After meals, I washed the dishes in the chilly river.

My Uncle Elzey had a few drinking buddies, and both were as old as dirt and knew these mountains like the back of their hands. My uncle would drop by to see what they were up to because when he went to the city, they would watch his place until he returned. We stopped by to see one of the old miners named Jed, and he was complaining that someone had stolen all the gold from his cabin. He was saving up a lot of gold dust in many bottles from a lifelong show of work. He couldn't report the theft because, at that time in the 1960s, it was illegal to hoard gold. Then we stopped by the other drinking buddy the following day, Sam, to get his report on how things were playing out with him. He was upset because the game warden discovered a lot of dead deer lying around his property that had been shot and left to rot. He tried to explain to the officer of the law that his dog would drag a dead deer home after a hunter shot it in the woods. You may have thought this was impossible until you saw the size of this dog. That dog walked in from the back of the cabin and looked me square in the eyes, and I was standing up. I would say this dog was the same height as me, which was four feet eight inches. If you would go by the metric system, it would be 1.72 meters. My uncle was a machinist, and he was teaching me this system he was using at work.

That small community had a post office, grocery store, hotel, and fire department. I went into the hotel to look around because it was said to be over a hundred years old and looked interesting. They had a signature at the hotel that they claimed was the original signature of a gunfighter named Bat Masterson. They claimed he stayed at this very hotel for a few days back in the Old West. I asked them if there were any kids in this town, and they said they hadn't seen one in a long while.

My uncle and I dug for a few weeks and found some small nuggets and gold dust. These mountains were dry and dusty and full of many old, abandoned mines that we would go into to explore. One of the mines, we found ourselves deep into the side of the mountain. It was very dark when we came to an end; my uncle said, "Shit, I hope there is no bear in here." I hoped that he was pulling my leg; however, I was ready to get my little butt outside.

Then, a few days later, we found another mine, which we had to wade through a few inches of water to get inside. It was dark, cold, and very creepy, and I was a little frightened. My uncle and I finally went back out, and I stopped to clean my shoes off at the front of the old mine. My uncle kept walking, then turned around, yelling at me to hurry up. I could hear his voice echo behind me inside the mine, causing it to collapse behind me; it was like an explosion. I started running, and the force of the collapsing cave pushed me into my uncle's arms as he said, "Holy shit, I didn't see that coming!" After that day, we never went back inside any other abandoned mines.

We did not give up looking for things, and minors left lots of junk behind. We found many old glass bottles and tin cups outside the mines in covered-up trash piles. I found a tin box with thousands of dollars inside, and it was a shame that it was Confederate money and not worth a dime.

The next day, I would play while my uncle slept in. My uncle was not a morning person; he usually would get up around noon and make breakfast.

I brought no extra clothes, and I needed a bath. The only water was the river and I had to use the woods for a restroom. This hole in a rock was alongside the trail, going past my uncle's property, which was shaped like a bathtub. I would fill this hole with river water and wait until the next day to take a worm bath and wash my clothes. After finishing, I knew how to drain the rock using a hose. I learned this by siphoning gas from our pickup truck to power our lawnmower.

I would lay on the rocks toasting my buns, waiting for my clothes to dry. My uncle told me to always keep my shoes on because of the rattlesnakes hiding under the rocks. I felt like I was back in Oklahoma while I was lying there catching the breeze, wondering what the girls were doing. Prospectors sometimes would walk by me because this trail goes through my uncle's property alongside the river, and only one group said anything to me. A lady walked by and put a bottle of tanning lotion next to my arm, saying kid, I think you need this more than me. I looked at her, saying thank you for the gift. Then I checked out my backend and said to her as she stepped off. Yes, things were looking toasty back there, and I thank you again.

This land belongs to my uncle, and they were trespassing. The next time I need a bath, I will put signs up at both ends of the trail in hopes of stopping the passersby. My uncle had many signs he intended to put up but never got around to them. He has excellent signs that say no trespassing, and one sign displays a shotgun.

I was once again laying there on my weekly bath, and wouldn't you know it, someone else was coming down the trail and ignoring my no-trespassing signs. I looked up to say hello to the intruders and was surprised by a gigantic bear. This big bear stood up with his paws, reaching for the sun and shouting a heart-stopping roar. This bear only saw the white butt of a boy streaking back up the hill to his uncle's cabin. I told my uncle what happened, and we returned to reclaim my clothes. The bear was gone, and so was my tuna sandwich. My uncle told me never to go off in the woods carrying food because the bears are hungry, and you look tasty to them. I hope he was joking about the part where I looked tasty to a bear.

While I was eating dinner with my uncle that night, I had to ask him something that had been troubling me for an exceptionally long time. I asked my uncle why my dad always kicked and slapped me. He would treat dogs better than me. When my dad looks at me, I only see anger in his eyes.

My Uncle Elzey told me that my dad was a wild child and was out of control. My uncle went on to say that my dad built a car out of wood and outran the cops across three states before they jailed him. My uncle told me my grandfather would kick the shit out of him for everything he did wrong, which turned out to be a lot. I asked my uncle if my dad was my father. My uncle said he knew nothing about that. However, my uncle told me if I bite back like a dog, he will think twice about harming me.

When I returned home to the city, the word got out about the bear and me. A friend of my uncle went up to that spot and killed the bear. I felt bad for the bear, for I thought this bear spared my life. I don't think I outran this bear because all that this bear needed was a tuna sandwich. The person who shot the bear got his name and picture in the newspaper, known as the Richmond Independent.

CHAPTER 10
RIVERSIDE ELEMENTARY

School was starting again, and to my surprise, my dad had been seeing doctors trying to get Social Security or what little he had coming to him. Mom said for a few months, Dad was seeing doctors, and they finally figured out what was wrong with him. The doctors said he had so much toxic heavy metal in his blood system he should have dropped dead years ago. Some doctors would define this as being lead poisoning. It's a metal that is used in car batteries and many other things, and too much of this in your system is deadly. Well, I couldn't be so lucky, so how do you deal with that? Put him out of his misery?

I remember the times he was pissed about the Army giving him shock therapy to the brain, and I guess they were trying to recharge his battery.

For the sixth grade, I went to Riverside Elementary, one of the nicest-looking schools I have ever attended. It was close to Wild Cat Canyon and a creek. There, I became friends with a boy who was like a brother I never had. Yes, I know I did have a brother; however, the way I was raised, he was just like a stranger. My at-home brother was a troublemaker, for he knew if he just squealed one time, my dad would sneak up and put his foot up my butt, saying, "Leave the God-damn baby alone." It only took a few kicks in the pie hole to get the message across, and it was loud and clear.

My new friend's name was Jack, and he was one of the most honest kids I have ever met. He and his family had moved out from Texas, and he had no fear and was hard as a rock. He never swore and believed in taking anything that wasn't his, and he knew how to defend himself without getting angry or dropping an ounce of sweat. The schoolyard bullies were no match for him, for if they tried to hit him, he would dodge every blow with a smile. He told me he won some boxing championships back in Texas, and his dad was a welder and had to move where the work was. This other kid in my class was also from Texas; his name was Joe Sillyowney, and I will never forget the day he brought his shotgun to school for show-and-tell. Of course, the school had his parents escort him back home with his twelve-gauge shotgun. I asked Mom if I could spend the weekend at my new friend's house, and after she said yes, I left her with Jack's phone number.

When I got to Jack's house, I found him living in the canyon, and his house was oddly sitting in a large creek. The foundation of this house was a tall concrete wall to protect this building from the water as it was washing by. Jack was in a little pond, paddling a bathtub around. I stripped my clothes off and joined him, and we had a lot of fun. We paddled the tub around for a while, and then we jumped in, played a little, and went back to the bank to put our clothes back on so he could show me around the rest of his property. This beautiful, tree-covered place could have fitted twenty more houses. The banks of this house in the hole were relatively high, with lots of ivy and poison oak. He had a motorcycle and even some rifles. This place was like being out in the wilderness. It was like I fell into a slice of heaven, a beautiful place located so close to the city.

He took me to the canyon on his dirt bike and was an expert at hill climbing. Then we went out and shot cans with his 22-caliber rifle. This kid had incredible marksmanship, hitting a bird out of the sky with one bullet. Most grown men couldn't do it with a large shotgun.

Jack made his can of New England clam chowder for dinner with a cube of butter, and it was the first time I had ever eaten that. Before bed, we jumped into a bathtub and started playing with his mom's water bottle. We had placed all our clothes into his mom's washing machine because they were muddy. Jack's mom was off with a friend, and when she got home, she stood at the bathroom door with a towel. She had us stand up, dried us off, Jack first, and then me as she told us to go to bed. I found myself trying to control myself, for somehow, my brain got connected to Binkie. I was trying not to embarrass myself, for puberty just showed up from nowhere as she was drying me off. Jack's mom's face reddened as I left her holding the towel, and if I had hung around any longer, she could have used Binky as a towel holder. We walked down a long hallway, then down some stairs leading to his room in the basement. When we got to Jack's room, he was kind enough to loan me some underwear until mine was finished drying. I was cold and quickly got under the cover because I made this long trip to his room without a towel or a robe. The cold air was what I needed, for it got Binkie back under control.

Jack's dad and his other two brothers were out late for a birthday party, so there were just the three of us in this big, old, dark, creepy house.

I didn't know we were going to church the next day, and I wore some holy-looking clothes as they dressed their boys up in suits and ties. We arrived at church, and I attended a Sunday School class with Jack. I was so embarrassed. I looked like a hobo compared to the children in the class. I was put into an embarrassing situation just because I needed a friend.

That afternoon, I walked back home, and it was a long walk. I saw Brother Strongs van coming down the road toward me, and I said, "Holy shit," as I jumped over a fence and hid in some bushes. Wouldn't you know it, he parked, got out, and was standing there looking at me lying in the bushes. He told me, "You never put in for a change of address. Would you like a ride home? However, it's a fine day for walking." He drove me home and spoke with my mom. Mom said I should go to church because I'm running out of soap with this boy. Brother Strong didn't know what she was referring to, and one day, he did ask, and I told him it was because my mom thought I had a potty mouth. Mom enjoys plugging my mouth with a soap bar when inappropriate words pop out. "Ronnie, I never heard you pop off a swear word, so why would your mother think you have a potty mouth?" "Well, sir, if you could have read my lips when you saw me walking up the road toward you that day, I'm sure the first stop before my house would have been the City's laundry room."

If I wasn't at Jack's house on weekends, I collected pop bottles, mowed lawns, or swept out parking lots. No one ever turned me down when I walked up to a store holding a broom, saying I will sweep your parking lot out for some cash. I liked finding broken-down bikes in the creek and rebuilding them. Monday through Friday, I did housework, and I kept an exceptionally clean house. I did all the ironing, wishing Mom would buy new clothes and not from a thrift store. I heard that the new garments were wash-and-wear and required no ironing.

When I went to Jack's house, I made it clear I would come from Friday to Saturday and not on Sunday. When I did stay at Jack's house, sometimes we would take wine out of his dad's shed and get drunk in the woods. On nights that we were plastered from shots of the hard stuff, we would go streaking throughout the neighborhood. We would set up camp in the canyon before the party so we would have a place to sober up so his parents wouldn't find out.

This went on until a cop found us passed out just off a side road with just our underpants on. The police officer told us to get in the back of the car and brought us to the police station. He only said one thing on the way to the station. He said, "I don't know if you boys have broken the law but have disturbed my peace. I had too many complaints from neighbors about you boys streaking throughout the streets wearing your underwear as a mask. Jack said in our defense, "You're wrong, officer. We were camping in the canyon, and it wasn't us." Then the officer replied to Jack, asking, "Do you boys always wear your underwear inside out? "We quickly fixed the problem before we got to the police station. However, our faces were as red as the police car lights and hot as his tailpipes.

It must not have been a busy day for this officer, for there was only one crazy woman locked up with us. The officer put me in this huge drunk tank and gave Jack a nice, comfortable cell. The police officer walks by Jack, who can't resist popping off, "Not too busy today, officer? Now resorting to locking up women and children?" I think Jack had a bit too much to drink, and he was pushing the officer's patients. I prayed that Jack wouldn't get me into more trouble than I just found myself in

They called our parents, and Mom came and got me. However, the policeman had to let Jack go because his parents told the officer he had two legs and could walk home. Of course, I told my mom we just stepped out of our sleeping bags when the cops nailed us in the canyon. I had plenty of time to think up a story on why I was in a police station just wearing a pair of whitey tidies.

My mom was angry because she was late for work. "Ronnie," she said. "When the policeman asked me, 'If this boy belongs to you? I almost said no! What mother picks her son up at a police station just wearing his underpants?" I thought to myself, the same mother that goes to work with two black eyes. I wished I could have told her how I felt, but I kept my big mouth shut; it wouldn't be good if I said anything. What would it change? I thought it was odd that the cops knew where I lived and even knew my phone number.

The next school day, Jack informed me that his dad beat the crap out of him when he got to the door. Jack walked me into the boy's bathroom and showed me the whelps on his back and legs from his dad's strap. I found out that Jack's dad was a hateful, mean drunk; however, he was able to hold down a job, so you call those kinds of critters functional alcoholics. That would explain the shed filled with nothing but wine and liquor. Our teacher overheard us talking about Jack's life at home as she was spying on us behind the bathroom door. This bathroom was very convenient for spying because it was located right across the hall from her classroom. Our sixth-grade teacher hated Jack and me; she must have been a little unstable. This woman would call Jack's dad with any little thing he did wrong, knowing he would get the crap beat out of him. It seemed to me that the two of them had their little personal war going on between them. In the first part of the school year, I paid a trip to the school nurse because my teacher plowed the boy's bathroom door open, almost knocking me out. A half dozen or more boys were in the bathroom, pissing all over the place. I didn't wish to get pissed on and made a run for a door, then, Bang! My teacher knocked me on the floor with that solid steel door, putting a large lump on my head. I was sent to the school nurse while the teacher spoke with the pecker-heads in the bathroom. The school nurse said, "It's not bad enough to take you to the emergency room." She told me it's in my school records that they couldn't contact my parents unless it were a life-or-death situation. I asked her,

"Does that mean you can't tattle on me?" She said, "I have no comment." I said what does that mean? She said, "Look it up in the dictionary when you return to class."

I was grateful to have a friend like Jack because we had something in common: both of us were abused by our father and could relate to some things we had to endure. I was also grateful that Jack taught me how to swim. At times, we would hitchhike to the Richmond Plunge, which was a huge indoor swimming pool. Jack would push me to the pool's deep end and say, "Swim or drown." I would come back doggie paddling, and he would keep pushing me away. At times, I was really upset with him because he would push me away from the edge of the pool and tell me not to dog paddle. He jumped in and showed me the sidestroke. I finally got the hang of it, and Jack said, "You can swim long distances using this method."

I loved standing in the showers for as long as I could, which was just one wall away from the walking area of the pool. A lady lifeguard would come into that shower area a few times and tell me it was time to close and get dressed. I would ask if she knew mouth-to-mouth because my friend was trying to drown me. They would get embarrassed that a kid would even ask that.

Once, a lifeguard lady said, "Hurry and return your rental so I can start closing." I said, "No problem, ma'am," The swimsuit was just hanging on the soap dish in the shower. As I handed it to her, she said, "Thank you, cutie." Then she turned the water off, spinning me around as she slapped my butt, pushing me out of the shower. She made my heart melt. It was better than what the other lifeguard said a few weeks before and called me "a little pervert." I loved this pool because the water was warm, and I would pull the same thing every time I was there with the lifeguards. The plunge rented swimsuits because cut-offs were not allowed in the pool, and you had to return them as you passed the office window. The staff would always rent me adult swimsuits that had leg openings as big as my waste. When I jumped off the diving board, I had to look for them and put them back on. I would watch the lifeguards, for I knew they were doing this intentionally to have some fun and laughter at my expense.

I never had a shower at home; it was just an old, dirty tub. However, there was endless hot water at the plunge, and I would always get my money's worth.

Jack would always order us food from the burger stand across the street from the plunge. When I caught up with him, it was ready and hot to eat. This burger stand made the best burgers in the East Bay. This little community was known as Point Richmond and was the home of a few historical landmarks. One of them was the Richmond Plunge, which opened in 1926. It was the largest indoor swimming pool in the United States during its opening day.

CHAPTER 11

THE BOMB

I almost blew the leg off Jack's desk with a bomb that I made during class. It was an accident. I did not think it would work. The principal gave me twenty lashes with a belt that was specially designed for total behind destruction. This leather belt was three inches wide and had holes in it, so there would be no air restriction when it was launched into action. Something like the science behind the holes in a fly squatter to deliver fast, accurate blows to the subject.

The clapping of Jack's metal desk leg on the floor sent my mind adrift. This classroom episode was one of many that the school had to endure. I was happy, contented, and a little sleepy because the school decided to pass me. Or did they do it to get rid of me, thinking I was some liability to them because of my father?

I had always wanted to make a bomb, but I didn't know how to or if I could even get the thing to work. I would spend a few weeks of school time scratching the gunpowder out of rolls of caps designed for a toy cap pistol. These caps made an excellent pop, along with a lot of smoke. It must have been five full boxes before I knew I had plenty of explosive powder. I carefully wrapped the aluminum foil around the gunpowder; the metal was easy for me to work with. I used a few staples out of the teacher's stapler and pretended that this would be my firing mechanism. I then wrapped the outer shell even tighter with more aluminum foil.

When I finished building this bomb, I waited for Jack to get up, and I was in luck because he needed another piece of paper. I placed the big oval thing under the back leg of his desk. Jack turned around and returned to his chair as I crawled from under his desk. I had carefully placed the bomb where I thought it would work the best. By some miracle, it worked! Jack dropped his skinny butt down on the seat of his chair as though it was a hammer. Boom! The explosion threw him off his chair, and smoke bellowed everywhere and out into the corridors. You could barely see anyone because the smoke was thick. Ms. Snout, our teacher, ran over and picked Jack up from the floor where the explosion had placed him. She said, "Are you all right?" She clenched him between the palms of her hands as she helped him up. It looked like a stork hovering over a newborn baby about to drop it into a nest. Trying to regain his bearings, Jack replied, "Yes, I'm all right." After he said that, her face turned into an angry buzzard as she began to shake him, saying, "You jerk! You stupid little punk jerk! You could have killed someone! "By then, the vice principal and principal stood in the doorway. They were only a few feet away from where I was sitting; I always sat next to the exit.

I couldn't bear to watch Jack take the blame. My friend was the only thing I had in this world. He was being shaken like a baby rattler, with his head and eyes bobbing all over the place. I realized I couldn't take it anymore and had to confess. I stood up and turned to the vice principal, saying, "Jack didn't do it. I did. I set the bomb off." "I made it; I didn't think it would work."

Vice Principal Barns grabbed me by the collar of my shirt and showed me the way out the door, with the lady principal following close behind. As we marched down the long corridor, it seemed like I was walking to the gas chamber, with the principal's chamber becoming more visible as our feet marched into a drum roll.

Many of the students were now out in the hall watching us walk by as though they were going to be witnessing an execution. The lady principal directed Mr. Barns to put me in a room as she went in first. Mr. Barnes was the size of a gorilla, as he stood with his back toward the door so I couldn't make a run for it. The principal turned around and looked at me with a mean stare and the wrath of judgment pulsating from the pupils of her eyes. I didn't see how I could say anything to my defense that would change anything, but I bet my big, fat mouth would make things worse.

The big, long fanny destructor was already hanging from her hand as she asked me, "Why did you do it?" I stood there and spoke. "Why did I do what?" She ran that line back at me, but this time in a real hostile tone of voice, "Why did you do it?"

I got worried then. I made up my mind that I was going to fight my way out by hitting Mr. Barnes in the stomach. I turned around, and he grabbed me like a sumo wrestler, forcing my arms against my chest. Now my butt was pointing at the principle for some cleansing of the soul with the use of the fanny destructor. Mr. Barns put me in an outstanding position for the principal to give it to me; he must have done this to some other poor souls. It seemed like grownups always like to take target practice on my butt. Except for my sickly little alcoholic dad, who didn't care what part of me he hit or kicked. None of the school officials wanted to be responsible for a life-threatening situation they might put me in by bringing any school problem to my dad. They had to do what was necessary at school to keep the peace and protect me from harm.

After ten swats, Mr. Barns put me back on the floor and stood me upright. The principal said to me, "Did you feel that?" I stood there looking into her eyes and said to her, with a voice of clarity, for they only pissed me off, "Feel what?" Shit, again, the wrong words just popped out of my mouth.

Before I knew it, Mr. Barns had me pinned back down on the floor with my face buried in the crotch of his pants. I did everything to free myself, and I even thought about sinking my sharp teeth into his leg. That was an old tactic I would use with my dad when we got into fights. It was a terrible struggle as Mr. Barns pinned my arms up against my chest; the principal ripped off my pants along with my underwear, and the counting started again. My attitude changed fast on that unexpected maneuver. I didn't expect them to display me in my birthday suit. I was struggling to get one hand free to retrieve my underwear that this principal used to lock my ankles together. Finally, after ten more slaps on my butt. Vice Principal Barns stood me back up as I retrieved my pants after I had unlocked my underwear to cover my butt. Then, they saw me doing what they wanted as I put my pants back on, along with one shoe that flew across the room. I was crying, and my face was red with embarrassment.

However, the principal just had to ask, "Did you feel that?"

Damn. I bit my lips and thought before speaking, which I rarely did, and I said, "Yes."

The principal asked me again as if she dared me to confront her with my words of unwisdom. I just nodded as tears went down my pink cheeks. I was marched back down to my classroom to apologize to everyone for what I did, and no one knew why I was crying, for the pain was nothing compared to what my old man could dish out. I was crying because I was embarrassed. I didn't know when I last put on some clean underwear.

The school bell rang as I came out of a daze, announcing the beginning of the last day of school. We were almost seventh graders, and we sat there. eager and happy about the day's events that we wouldn't have to repeat. Well, at least I hoped I had passed the sixth grade.

We sat quietly in class as our teacher gave us her last glare. She was making it quite clear how much she hated us by sweeping her flaming hawkish eyes around the room. She probably wished she could burn us at the stake as if we were little witches and warlocks. If she could have gotten away with the massacre, she would have tied us up right there in our seats without hesitation.

This was her way of showing us how glad she was to see us move on since most of us were troubled children from troubled homes. It was also her way of keeping her sanity, for she was caught between school officials and something called credibility, for this was her first year of teaching a classroom filled with kids.

We didn't like her because she was so different from the rest of us. She was mean, hated children, and said things you wouldn't expect from a teacher. Once, I asked Ms. Snout for a straw for my milk, and she told me if I stuck it in my nose, it would come out my ear because, "Ronnie, you have no brain in there." Well, now it's all behind us of what she said, and all will be behind us of what we did to her.

Jack turned around, almost falling off his now crippled chair. He turned back around quickly so Ms. Snout wouldn't notice him. Then, when she wasn't looking, Jack turned back around and said, "Let's cut school at lunchtime." I nodded my head as I was responding in approval.

I was always a follower and not a leader. We crawled out through the hole in the back chain link fence. We found ourselves at the canyon cliff and yelling at the top of our lungs, denoting all the school officials in profanity." We grew tired of that and found ourselves walking alongside a large highway. Jack came up with another idea and called it "Drive-by-mooning." We received a lot of motorists honking at us as though they were cheering us on. We were shaking our butts at the passersby and causing a traffic jam. I noticed one was an officer of the law. His eyes were hypnotized as though he was a deer looking at two bright headlights as it was shining at him in the dark of the night. "Shit," I said as we pulled our pants up and made a run for it. It was getting late, and I told Jack that I had to return to school before the bus left or they would notify the authorities. More than likely, it would be the same cop that was checking us out, except he would now have a name attached to my butt.

Jack was upset with me but did as I asked, and we returned to school. Jack didn't have to take the bus to school, and he didn't have to come with me, but he did. We went back through the hole in the chain-link fence and guess who was standing up high on the school's loading platform. It was the principal with her arms crossed and her face as red as an apple, ready to explode into applesauce. She said the only thing she could say in anger as she watched us walk by in shame, saying, "Did you boys have a nice day at the park?" I ran to the bus because the driver stood outside the folding door waiting for me. I got on the bus and found a seat while I watched the principal come up and speak with the driver. The driver took off and sent a classmate telling me the driver said you must take a seat right behind him. When he got to the bus stop, he ordered me to stay on the bus and took me to my house. His last stop was just for me and only me like I was VIP. That was the last day I ever set foot in an elementary school.

A few weeks later, Jack called and said they were moving out of the state. He did say the pipelines his dad was working on were finished. I wished him the best and told him to always remember the night we cut our thumbs and became blood brothers for life. He told me he'd never forget me. He said they might be going back to Texas and would try to call me once they landed.

Jack told me that he and his dad had come to an understanding. You know, a come-to-Jesus' moment. Jack's dad ordered him out in the yard to take another beating, and when his dad cleared the house, Jack shot the strap out of his hand. Jack told his dad that if he ever hit him again, the next bullet would be between his eyes. Jack's dad got the message and threw the strap at Jack's feet.

I was happy for Jack because I once witnessed a brutal beating that Jack received from his dad. Jack's dad wildly slapped him all around the yard with an unbelievably large strap. I thought that his dad was going to kill him and that I would be a witness to a murder. When his dad launched himself out of the door, this giant ape went insane, continuously beating on him. I was in shock seeing this and ran for home.

With Jack gone, I wanted to catch up on some of my favorite television shows. Some were old reruns. However, they never got old. I would watch them all, and my favorite was Lassie. I felt I could play the kids' part and do a better job. I thought this boy looked like me enough to be my brother.

The only solid upbringing I ever received was through the aid of television shows. I would put myself in the child actors' shoes to receive the affection and guidance I was missing in my life.

There were some television shows I should have avoided, and one was 'The Three Stooges.' It was a not-so-good influence on a kid who didn't watch his sugar intake. It would get my butt whipped in school, or at times I would find myself with my nose poking in the corner of the classroom.

CHAPTER 12

DELL MONTE DRIVE

A few more weeks went by, and Mom told me the government granted Dad his social security, and we were moving to a newly built home in a housing development called Bay View. One might think it was in Pinole, a middle-class area; however, it was still considered San Pablo. This was an unincorporated area next to San Pablo Bay and on the other side of the railroad tracks from Pinole. Everyone was getting ready to make the move by getting rid of the junk piled up in the yard and some old pickups that did not run. Besides being a drunk, Dad collected junk to tinker with.

Dad also bought a new pickup truck that was a powerhouse and could hall anything. We went to look at the new house and did a walkthrough. I was so happy, seeing things I had never seen before. The carpet was beautiful, just lying on the floor. It was the first time I had the pleasure of walking on carpets except for the inside of a church. I sat on the carpet, looking at the popcorn ceiling while praising God. This house had a wood-burning fireplace and a thing called garbage disposal. This new home had an attached garage and a nice, clean, beautiful shower in the bathroom. No new homes were finished across the street so that you can see the beautiful San Pablo Bay. The house was within walking distance of a little beach at the bay, and everything now was so different. I walked along this little sandy beach, recording memories by inhaling the smell of the Bay's water. I felt my prayers were answered.

We moved in, and the new home smell was exciting and wonderful. Our new next-door neighbors moved in a few days later, and one was a cop. Well, that would put a stop to Dad's drunks and beating on me and my mother unless he would like to go to jail. I went down to the bay and played in the waters, and it was nice and not too cold. This was city life, and I never owned a bathing suit, so I ripped off the legs of my pants and made some shorts to swim in. It was not hard to do, for I just put my finger in the holes already there and let them rip. Well, it almost worked because part of my goods was hanging out. No problem. I returned to the house, got a different pair of pants, and located a pair of scissors.

My dad's sister, Aunt Dean, lived in Santa Barbara and married into a well-off family. She had two boys a little older than me, and I would only see them at Christmas when they visited my grandmother. One day I found five large boxes of her boys' clothes on my front porch that they grew out of and were almost new. I was grateful for what she sent me, especially the long shirts you didn't have to stick into your pants. This was important to an adolescent boy who had just turned twelve. These items were bought in major high-class department stores, and I had never been to a high-class department store. Well, the first time I was in a department store came later before school because mom had to buy me gym clothes for now; I was in the seventh grade. We drove to a place called Woolworth, a department store located on the main drag of Richmond, California. As we pulled up and parked, you could smell the aroma of popcorn as it drifted out through the store's front door. This was my first time being in a high-class department store, and I was embarrassed. Mom pulled a jockstrap out of the box and waved it around, saying, "You think it will fit?" That was the first time I had received a thing called a jockstrap. The shirt was bright yellow, the shorts were a nice red, and the jockstrap was snow white. I was extremely grateful that my Aunt Dean sent me a lot of nice clothes to wear to school. It was something different and new to me.

More new homes were being built, and I hoped a few kids would move in so we could play in the bay's waters. However, moving to this new area cost me my source of income. There were no discarded pop bottles or parking lots to sweep, and everyone had a lawn mower.

Summer went by fast, and on the first day of school, I sat in a classroom with butterflies in my stomach. This middle school was high up on the hill from San Pablo Bay, and the school playground faced overlooking the water. The name of this school was Pinole Junior High, and it was well-kept, not rundown or too old. I looked around and was puzzled, looking at the children in the classroom. Most of the children were white, well-dressed, middle-class kids. I have never attended a school with almost a hundred percent middle-class children. I did not make any friends in school. However, three boys in my first-period class liked to pick on me for some odd reason, so I just let them have their fun. I just wanted to stay out of the eyes of the school's authority.

In the seventh grade, you are required to dress down for physical education every day, and I was lucky that this was one of the schools that did not have showers. One of these three troublemakers from my first-period class dropped my gym shorts past one of my shoes as I stepped up. I stepped right out of my shorts and fell on my face. I was lying there, exposing my white butt to everyone in the class. I got up, turned around, and was going to punch him in the face. I pulled back because I did not wish to become best friends with the principal again. His other two friends tossed my shorts into the basketball hoop, right into the net. I was franticly shaking the pole, trying to get them down while the crack of my ass was catching the breeze from the Bay. The rest of the class laughed and cheered when my shorts floated back down. I hopped back into my shorts and told these jokers I would deal with them later. Our gym teacher would take roll call and have us pull our jockstraps out from under our shorts to see if we were dressed according to regulations. Then, after a few calisthenics, the instructor would disappear. This gave the three stooges the run of the place, and they did anything they wished.

You know that day did come. I found all three of the boys down on the rock at the bay. I put my fists up and said, "Come on, let's do this," as I started yelling many words of profanity at them. I ran toward them like a mad dog as they ran back across the railroad tracks like little cowards. I do not know what happened. I looked behind me, thinking maybe someone other than me had frightened them off. I knew they could have wiped my little butt all over that rock. Now, the boys gave me some respect at school and left me alone.

Around eight weeks into the school year, I was chilling in the school's lunchroom. I was approached by a cafeteria worker asking me if I could help wash the lunch trays because she claimed her helper had not shown up. This job pays with an all-you-can-eat lunch. I always had a problem saying no, so I did it for the entire year instead of playing at recess. I had no friends anyway, so this dishwashing machine, which I named Colleen, became my only school friend. I wonder if school officials targeted me to get me into this job so I would have lunch every day. Or maybe they looked at my school records and thought they should watch this one.

My grades were ok, just average for this school. This school only passed you if you earned it. When the school bell rang, I would always run the two miles home, for it was all downhill, and I was excited to see if there was anything new at home.

The school wanted me to be on the track team. However, I knew that would cost money, and I said no thank you. My physical education teacher told me that if my parents had a problem, he would talk to them so I could be on his team. I was the fastest kid he had ever seen who could run a mile while breaking all middle school records. I kindly said no, and it would never work out. I remember the last time a teacher came to my house, and it did not have a fairy tale ending.

Halloween came around, and I did not have a costume. I stood there looking at myself in the bathroom mirror, thinking, "What could I be?" My hair was long, and I desperately needed a haircut. My hair covered my ears and was just above my eyebrows. I thought I looked like a girl. So that was the solution to my problem. I would go out dressed as a girl. I just borrowed my sister's clothes and my mom's shoes and there you have it, a free costume. I looked cute in my plaid skirt, white laced panties, and black shoes. Yes, my sister even helped me transform myself from boy to girl. I would go door to door, and they would tell me I had to have a costume to get some candy. I would tell them I was a boy dressed as a girl; it was not fun because they thought I was lying to them.

My neighbor across the street had to take a second look and had me do a spin for him. My skirt made his face smile as I displayed my ruffled-up laced undies while performing my spin. "I know who you are," he said. "You're that little slave boy that lives across the street." I said, "That's me." He sat down on the swing on his porch, and so did I. We were looking at my house across the street. He said, "You guys fixed the yard up nicely. Where did you get all the rocks?" I told him they came from the mountains close to a town called Washington. My neighbor said his name was Jared, and he retired a year ago. He told me he saw what happened when my dad was drilling something out of the ground and was being electrocuted because the drill shorted out. He said he started running across the street to help, and your housebreaker must have tripped.

I said, "Yes, I know. I was standing there watching, and he was upset with me because I didn't pull the plug." My dad asked me, "Boy, what is wrong with you?" I pissed him off when he crawled back into the house when I said, "Remember, I'm not your boy." My neighbor was a little confused at what I said and asked me, "You mean slave boy, son?" I did not wish to get into the whole story, so I just said, "Yes, sir, something like that." I said it was getting late, and I still had some candy to collect. He said good luck, and we would talk later.

I was by myself, depressed. I had no friends in the neighborhood, so I thought I would start some trouble. I took my hot skirt and went out, flashing the boys showing off my ruffled-up panties while shaking my butt. The next thing you know, I had a group of boys behind me looking for the wrong candy. I turned around and had to confront the boys. I said, "I hate to pop your bubble because I am a boy." That got rid of most except for two high school boys who said, "We can live with that babe." One boy pushed up behind me, putting his hands on my fake boobs and giving them a good squeeze while his friend in front of me sniffed the perfume from my neck. I screamed like a girl, pushed them off me, ran up the street, and found a classmate dressed as Snow White. I asked her mom if I could hang with them because the boys down the street were teasing me. She said, "No problem, sweetie, just stay close to us." We went door to door and became good friends, and I wasn't going to spoil the moment by telling them I was a boy. They had no clue that I was not a girl. Snow-white told me her name was Kathy, and I knew it because she was in my math class at school. She asked me what school I attended. I told her my name was Caroline, and I was home-schooled. However, I do have a twin brother that attends your school. We came to their house, and Kathy's mom invited me in for a little cake. I just sat there enjoying the cake and let them do all the talking. Kathy showed me her room and all the softball trophies and other achievements she was awarded as we sat on her bed. Unexpectedly, Kathy got up and removed her dress. Then she went looking for her nightgown, talking to herself, "Where did mom put it?" It seemed to have taken her more than five minutes to locate her gown, and when she found it, I could see why, for it wasn't much bigger than a scarf. My eyes were on fire, and my skirt was slowly elevating, so I had to stand up quickly to hide the situation. Kathy did not have a bra on, and her breasts were perfect and perky. She had a fantastic figure as I watched her walk around in a skimpy pair of laced panties with a lovely black bowtie above her cute camel toe. I knew she was talking a lot, but I didn't hear a word she said. I was petrified, and my heart was pounding out of my chest. While watching her, I realized she was more into girls than boys. I said I must go because it was getting late, and I was worried that the bulge forming under my skirt might become noticeable. Kathy forced me up against her door when I was making my escape and started making out with me as her tiny little nightgown floated to the floor. I made my escape when she retracted her tongue out of my mouth. It was beautiful to feel her hot boobs up against me, and I desperately wanted it, and she knew it. If I had let it go too far, she would find out I'm a wolf in sheep's clothing. I pushed her off me so I could make my escape and would have loved to have stayed. However, she would have gotten a big surprise, and then my butt would probably be in juvenile hall. My pantyhose were extremely tight, and now they were becoming unbearable. If it weren't for my tight pantyhose, I would have popped my cork in Kathy's room and destroyed my sister's clothes. Kathy's mom met me at the front door, kissed me on the cheek, and hugged me as I went out their door. Kathy's mom must have known her daughter was making out with me, for Kathy's lipstick was plastered all over my face. Her mom smiled at me as I left, winking and saying, "Come back soon, sweetie." I rushed up the street for an emergency adjustment because the pantyhose was cutting off something I wanted to keep. My balls were in pain, and it felt like they were trying to crawl up into my kidneys.

I must give my sister credit for helping me with this project. Maybe she overdid it because I even had a pretty blue headband with a lovely little flower on one side. I was always worried about some things I did, pushing it too far and getting my butt thrown into jail.

I had to call it a night because things were not going how one would expect, and I still had two high school boys tailing my hind end. I was puzzled about why they were still stocking me and was a little frightened. I stayed away from the bushes just in case they tried to pounce on me. I returned to my house, and they followed me to my front door. Jared was watching the high schoolers and told them to go home. I turned around and gave Jared a wave as if I were saying thank you. As I went back inside my house, I thought, "Crap! I hope that wave did not look too weird. I found myself depressed, looking in the bathroom mirror and wondering if this was why my dad hated me. I look like an odd duck compared to his other sons. My teeth were perfect, and my complexion was maybe too girly. I jumped into the shower and washed the high liner off my eyes; I kept my eyes closed with the worm water pouring at the back of my neck as I replayed my favorite parts of the night. It was an exceptionally long shower, and the water got cold, which brought my mind back out of the drain. I washed the layer of soap off the wash rag, dried myself off, and went to bed. I tried to get some sleep. However, school would be in session the next day, and I forgot to remove the nail polish from my toes. I didn't wish to show up for physical education class again with nail polish on my toes. This was one of the jokes my sister played on me. I always sleep like a rock with my socks on, and one night, she painted my toes a lovely bright pink and put my socks back on. I was embarrassed the next day when I changed my socks in my P.E. class. However, I wasn't the only boy with painted toes. One boy always had his toes and fingernails painted black and wore his jockstrap throughout the day. However, he wasn't alone; other boys wore jockstraps to different classes throughout the school year. I always sat in the back of the class, and it was too obvious when they bent over. I'm pretty sure that all the boys in this school have kept their jockstraps on after class at one time or another.

A few weeks later, I met some boys playing in the waters at the bay, and one became my best friend. He had other best friends, so it was fun when he had time for me. We would swim, jump off the cliff into the sand for thrills, and go on long walks alongside the railroad tracks, which ran alongside the bay. He went to a private school, and so did his other friends. There were also girls in the neighborhood, and now they just stayed away from me. The girls here were upper class and taught to avoid boys looking for romance. The ladies were different from the neighborhood girls I left on University Avenue.

There was a fisherman who would wait until the tide went out to drop his line and then wait for a big one as the tide returned. One day, it happened; he hooked over a six-hundred-pound sturgeon, pulled it in, and got his face and fish in the newspaper. The newspaper wrote that no one had ever caught a sturgeon of that size while fishing from land.

There was a large field where people would dump things next to our housing track, and I would check it out to see if there was anything of interest. My physical education class was the last period, and this school had no shower requirements. On Fridays, I would run home wearing gym shorts, drop my stuff off at the house, and return to the field. I would always pass by this field on my way home from school, and if I saw something of interest, I would come back looking. I was looking at a few items of interest on this dirt road, and a white

Chevrolet station wagon pulled up beside me. It was the fisherman who caught the sturgeon, and I said high. He got out and showed me his fish in the back, all cut up like stakes in large boxes. I guess it was fish, for I had never seen anything like the stuff in the back of his wagon. He said, "I have so much I'm giving it away. Do you think your mom would like some fish?"

I always had a problem saying no and thought she would like some fish. This fisherman was known because he got his picture in the paper along with his big ugly fish. The fisherman said, "Great, get in, and let's give her some fish. I jumped into the seat of his car, finding myself having to dig the strap of my slingshot out of the crack of my butt. I noticed the fisherman's eyes had drifted over, checking me out. The school gym shorts were as short as you could get them without exposing your goods just standing up.

I believed a voice came to me, saying I was in danger, and fear came over me. Why would someone be out in a large, isolated field with a carload of chopped-up fish? There was a stench of death inside this meat wagon, and I didn't think it was fish. The car started moving, and so did his hand. This fisherman grabbed me by the back of my shorts while I ejected myself out of his station wagon. I found myself on the side of the dirt road, pulling my shorts back up to cover my butt. I was dazed and didn't know what to think, for this fisherman kept going with the passenger door swinging open. I was frightened because my dad would kick the crap out of me if the police showed up at our house. I didn't know if this fisherman was trying to keep me safe by not letting me jump out of a moving car or if some evil intentions were at play.

This must have been a dangerous spot for my final junk gathering when someone tried to kill me. I was out looking for more exciting junk on a weekend when a bullet whizzed through the hairs at the top of my head. Sadly, I pissed in my shorts as I ran for cover. There was no time to stop and take a leak; it could have been my last one. However, let me tell you, I never went back looking for free junk again. Word got out that two girls were murdered execution-style on the rock at the bay. Without question, I believe this person was trying to kill me, for I must have gotten too close. One of the girls was the principal's daughter of an elementary school. Yes, the same one who called the cops on my father when he kicked me and broke my rib.

Throughout the school year, I played with my friend Bill when he was not busy with the other friends he had. One fine morning, we thought we would go to the next town by going up the railroad tracks. We came to a blind spot as we walked up the tracks with the wind blowing heavily against our backs. This bend went around a dirt-filled bank to where you could not see anything coming at you. I grabbed Bill, throwing us both off the tracks, screaming, "A train is coming!" I thought I would try to put the fear of God in Bill; it was supposed to be just a joke. Just at the same time as I did that, a passenger train flew by, and Bill started hugging me as we were lying on the ground, thanking me for saving his life. I kneeled, thanking God for his protection; it was indeed a brush of death. Bill continued shivering with fear, and I believed this kid was about to go into shock or he had an asthma problem. I tried to get him back down to planet Earth. I looked at Bill and said, "It was not me; it was God. Do you understand Bill? Bill, for some odd reason, it seems, and I do not know for sure, I may have angels protecting me." Did I have angels protecting me? Could my Aunt Betty's prayers be so powerful in the eyes of God? It had to be because, too many times, my life was put in danger, and yet a turn of events saved me. I believe that angels exist, and the only demon you must worry about is the one you let into your soul.

Around Easter, a man in our neighborhood asked my mother if he could take my sister and me to church. I found myself kneeling at the altar, thanking God for the change: new home, new school, and the police officer who lived next door. I put in another request for help with a slight problem. You see, my mind may fall into the gutter once too often, and I may need some help with that little issue. I want to thank you, Jesus, for your protection in the situations I have gotten myself into. Word came to my sister that the churchgoer we now knew as Kevin was in a motorcycle accident. My sister got information from Mom on what hospital he was in, so we picked some wildflowers to bring to him. He was at Doctors Hospital in Pinole, close to my school, so we hiked up the hill together. We let the head nurse know that we came to pray for Kevin, and they allowed us to enter the room. At first, we were both shocked when we walked into his room. Kevin was lying there in an entire body cast that covered most of his head. We walked up to him, put the flowers on the stand, laid hands on him, and prayed. He never said anything; I did not even know if he could. We left him as he was, shedding a lot of tears. That was the last time we ever saw Kevin.

CHAPTER 13

THE LAST RIDE

I turned thirteen a few days after finishing seventh grade, and my Aunt Dean sent me a bus ticket to go to Santa Barbara and work as a carnie. My Uncle Bill and Aunt Dean owned a carnival called Wes Shows.

When school was out, they would travel from city to city, making money using their mobile amusement park. I thought I had been blessed with a new home and a good school. Now, I am on an adventure of a lifetime to work in a carnival.

When I got to Santa Barbara, I found a beautiful city with many well-off people and movie stars living by the ocean. My cousin Steve said the following day, "Let's go swim in the ocean." Then he tossed me a pair of oversized gym shorts and a jockstrap that could hold the brains of Godzilla. I thought to myself that these people had the money, and yet they could not afford swimsuits. While I was getting dressed, and then wouldn't you know, Steve pulled out a swimsuit from his bedroom cabinet just for him. I was folding my clothes on my cousin's bed, leaving my underwear on top of the pile. Steve said, "It looks like my mom even sent you my old underwear." I was slightly embarrassed because his initials were still marked over the brief's label. A well-known brand that was called "Fruit of The Loom." I don't know which was more embarrassing. The label calling my goods a bowl of fruit, or his name was still marked on the briefs with a permanent marker. My Aunt had two boys and labeled everything, so she knew what belonged to whom.

We were finally ready and dressed and off to see the ocean. His bedroom had a door, like a second backdoor of the house, so we didn't have to sneak out through a window. After a long walk, we finally reached the beach, which Steve said some movie stars think they own. However, the government owns the beach up to the high-water mark.

We went swimming, and I went out too far from the shore, and the tide quickly brought in something I had never seen before. Steve wasn't watching, and I found myself in a school of seaweed.

Steve was now yelling at me to float on my back to get out of the seaweed or I would drown. I knew nothing about the dangers of the ocean, and someone should have filled me in before I tested the waters. I didn't realize the nature of my predicament until I got back to shore and saw what I swam out of. I then realized I was too overly confident in my swimming capabilities. After that near brush of death, we returned to the house after Steve got his thrill for the day.

I did not see any movie stars; if I did, I would give them my middle finger. No movie star was going to force me off government property. I felt that the U.S. Army failed to pay for the harm they placed upon me by letting my dad out of their nut house. I was upset one day thinking about the crap I had to put up with, and I sent the Pentagon a bill for two million dollars. The person who opened that bill probably laughed his butt crack off.

The next day, we all went to the storage yard, where all the carnival rides had been stored for the winter. Then, we started the diesel trucks and left for Santa Paula to set up the carnival. I found my seat was now, and always will be, next to my Uncle Bill in the eighteen-wheeler semi. I have never ridden in a truck of that size, and when you are the passenger, you hope the driver knows how to operate it. When we got there, we set up a few large lights and dropped this trailer off because it was a generator that provided electricity to all the lights and rides. We worked all night dropping off trailers and returning to the yard to pick up more rides.

My uncle had three semi-trucks and many trailers to move from one place to another. My uncle had the cleanest carnival in the country. It was mandatory that the employees who were hired had to have clean criminal records. My Uncle Bill was very protective of his two boys, and now, he had to protect his thirteen-year-old nephew. He made me feel like I was his son, and he was like a father I wish I had. Uncle Bill was funny, intelligent, and kindhearted; however, he looked like he could beat your ass if you crossed him.

I told my uncle about my problem with my dad and that the doctors finally figured out what was wrong with him. I said to my Uncle Bill, "I wished the Army would have just kept him; he was mentally ill and crazy. My dad is like a vegetable." I said, "Dad never says anything to me unless he is angry, drunk, or just wishes to bark orders at me. I am his personal slave. We moved next door to a cop, and for now, he stopped beating my mother and me." Then I said to my uncle. "My mother never talks to me much about anything and is a noticeably quiet person. She is often worn out working in the restaurant and sometimes pulling double shifts. You know she has never hugged me or even said she loves me. I think that is so weird. What am I? Just a piece of furniture?"

My Uncle Bill told me he fought for this country and was a machine gun operator on a tank. He told me that it took a few years of healing before his nightmares would stop. Sometimes, at night, he would almost kill Aunt Dean because of his dreams. He said, "When you let that machine gun roll, I would cut the enemy in half. I would watch their little legs run down the hill after I saw their bodies off with the use of my machine gun. War can make a grown man cry and even make you go insane."

I told Uncle Bill about the time my dad ripped off my sister's pet chicken's head, laughing and watching her run around headless until she dropped dead. My dad only did this because he gets intense pleasure by putting fear and anger in my mind. I knew he was looking at me with a smile from Hell, laughing and dancing like someone who should be put away in the nut house for life.

Finally, the day came when everything was ready as the huge diesel power generator was powered up, bringing all the carnival rides to life. We tested all the rides to ensure they were safe, and my uncle showed me how to operate the astronaut ride. I was assigned to work on this ride, which looked like something I could handle. This ride would let the passenger control the capsule's motion on their command as the ride went around in circles. They can make it go up or down; however, if I hit the switch, they will all fall gently down to the ground at once. This ride was strong enough for parents to ride with their children, and I found that some mothers liked going commando. These VIP mothers would get an extra-long ride as I dropped the capsule on my command. I tried not to make it look so obvious when I hit that switch, trying to get a little peak.

This was the best ride ever, and as I was standing there drooling, my uncle tapped me on the shoulder and said, "Would you like to work the candy wagon?" I stood there with a cute little smile until I realized what he was implying. My mind would play in the gutter until it returned to reality. At times, I felt like I had this other brain that was in control, and it wasn't located on my shoulders. I should have asked God again to help me with this harmless slight problem before I embarrassed myself. My Uncle Bill wanted to close the ride down to replace some lights; he was proud of his business. This was the best ride in the carnival, and the day flew by when I was the operator. One VIP mom slid off and said, "Too bad you didn't have a camera." I thought that was an excellent idea. I could capture that moment and sell some pictures. Then, thinking it through, maybe it's not a good idea, and I will wind up embarrassing myself.

We went from city to city, and what fun people had when they got on my uncle's rides. We would visit beautiful cities like Dana Point, Long Beach, Santa Rosa, and Santa Paula. Sometimes, I had to help my aunt in the candy wagon making corn dogs and cotton candy and would make some for myself. I was paid weekly and spent my money on food and clothing.

I made enough money to support myself after taxes. My uncle would take out a little to help with a hotel room so we could shower; however, most of the time, we would sleep in the trailers. I loved the bean burritos sold in some towns, but only if they had freshly chopped onions and lots of cheese. Some of these cities and towns we went to were just unbelievable regarding the wealth that some would have. I like Dana Point; it's a beautiful beach with extremely expensive homes alongside the water.

We set up the rides within walking distance of Dana Point and had one day of rest before the fun started. I went down to the beach with the rest of the crew and rented a surfboard, and again, I should have been worn about the dangers of the ocean. I took my surfboard out to catch a wave, and I did, except that slippery board shot off, leaving me behind. I did not know you had to tie the board off to your foot. It was a long swim back, and the weight of my pants was dragging me down. The lifeguards were too busy checking out the topless girls with their breasts stuck in the sand. Maybe I should have yelled for help, but instead, I said to myself that I would rather drown.

I had no choice; I left my pants in the ocean, for it was a life-or-death struggle to return to the beach. While walking back up the beach, I still had my long white T-shirt, and a kind lady handed me her towel, saying, "Kid, we have rules on this beach." I thanked her, and maybe I showed a few tears of gratitude. I returned the surfboard and walked back to the carnival. The next day, I returned and found that at least my pants had made it back to shore. My new boxers will have to be chalked up as a loss because they were still hanging onto an offshore rock.

On the last day, at Dana Point, my Uncle Bill and I walked to the store for some things to buy for the candy wagon. The grocery store had a laundromat next door, and it was a beautiful sunny day for a walk. We were walking by; this lady bent over, playing with her basket of dirty clothes, which she dragged out of the trunk of her car and placed on the pavement. This gorgeous woman was bent over, purposely exposing her curly bush to me. My Uncle Bill roared as we walked by, "Quick, kid, stick your finger in it.!" It didn't faze this lady at all about what my uncle said, and she just wiggled it a little more.

I was embarrassed and relieved at the same time. Maybe I am normal after all. It was the most embarrassing time of my life because my uncle knew that this thirteen-year-old boy wanted to finger the pie. I was weak at the knees and trying to reach the store door when my uncle said you could tell she's not a natural blond. I had never fainted in my life, but I felt like it may happen. Then my uncle couldn't let it go and said, "Did you see the outhouse on that hussy?" I said, "Please, Uncle Bill, you're killing me."

We got what we needed, and it was a lot of hotdogs for my aunt to make corndogs for the upcoming location. We were heading back across the parking lot, and the hussy's car was still there. My Uncle Bill said, "Ronnie, let me ask you a spiritual question." Uncle Bill had a big grin on his face, and I thought to myself, well, this can't be good. My uncle said, "Ronnie, you attended church a lot, and I had a thought that had been bothering me for a long time," He whispered the question in my ear, and my face turned red as a traffic light. I told my Uncle Bill you must ask God himself about that. I wondered if my uncle was giving me that father-son talk I never received from my dad. However, my uncle was doing an excellent job of trying to provide me with a nervous breakdown.

The next day, we packed up and arrived at a different location. I woke up that following day from sleeping in the Astronaut trailer and could not move my head. I could not straighten my neck, and if I tried, there was tremendous pain that would register in my brain. My aunt took me to the emergency room, and the doctors gave me some pills to help dissolve the blood clot in my neck. I do not know how much that cost them. I realized now that I had become more of a liability than an asset. My aunt found out with a phone call to my mom that I had no medical insurance, and I was in their care, so what could you do but send me back to where they found me?

It was time to return home, so my aunt put me on a bus and shipped me back to the Bay Area. In a way, it was like the school district I was in. I was more a liability than an asset. I wondered when Mom would try and get rid of me. I am sure she will try when she finally thinks I am more of a liability than an asset.

CHAPTER 14
WILCOX STREET

Mom came to pick me up at the bus station and brought unwelcome news. Mom told me we moved back down the hill, and I would now attend a middle school on the border of San Pablo and Richmond. That school was known to have troubled children from the ghetto who carried switchblades and brass knuckles. This school had showers, and you had to shower every day before leaving the physical education building. That alone brought fear to me, being vulnerable to well over thirty unruly boys in a gang shower. What was the difference between that and being in prison?

This was the 1960s, a time of civil unrest, and rumors of riots occurred in some East Bay schools. This school was in a bad area, where you had better keep your front door locked. I was crying inside, so upset and disturbed. I asked, "Why, Mom?" She said the county believed I should have paid the money to them when Dad received his backpay from the Social Security office. The county said we had to sell the house to pay my medical bills. Then she told me the county folks changed their mind, saying we did not have to sell. Mom said it was too late because she had signed a contract with the real estate people. The real estate agent informed Mom that to back out of the contract, she was still required to pay them the commission. Mom did not have the commission, so she was forced to sell the house.

As we left the bus station, I thought I would never see my friends again. I did not know if I had destroyed our friendship by running off like a coward. Bill, Barnie, and I were at the Bay when a slow-moving train was passing by carrying many new automobiles. Bill could not resist and started smashing out as many windows as possible. A man walked up as the train finished passing and told us he was with the railroad authorities and would have to spank our butts or turn us over to the railroad police. He demanded that we turn around, line up, drop our shorts, and take the whipping. I went to get a closer look at him, and it was the fisherman. I freaked out and ran home as fast as possible, leaving my friends to deal with this creepy dude. This is when I caught the bus to Santa Barbara. I just hoped my friends followed my lead and got out of there.

The neighborhood we left was probably grateful for this family leaving the Bay View area. For me, on the last day of school, Kathy asked me if she could sign my yearbook. I told her I didn't have one. Kathy said that's ok; I will sign the back of your T-shirt. She wrote, using a marker, "Caroline, have a lovely summer; my mom is going to cut off your little pink balls and feed them to our dog." Kathy would have never figured out who that girl was on Halloween night if my sister Carol hadn't become her brother's girlfriend. However, that Halloween night, I learned the meaning of blue balls and how painful they can get. It was a weird Halloween, and I discovered it could be dangerous for a twelve-year-old boy to go out dressed as a girl. Kathy should have been grateful that I kept her little secret. It was probably why she kept quiet until the last day of school.

My sister Carol, short for Caroline, was credited for setting the large field on fire, and it took over four fire department trucks to keep the fire away from our housing track. The high, dry grass and strong bay wind helped raise the Devil from the ground. My sister told the police she was sharing a smoke when her boyfriend threw it into the grass. Later, my sister told me a different story about what had happened. She told me she was trying to light up a cigarette and dropped the match in the grass.

Then there was my brother. He and his little buddies managed to break into a neighbor's house and were caught by the police. Not to mention the other time, they spray-painted their names on someone's house. How can you be that stupid?

I often wondered why boys would destroy buildings, break windows, and set things on fire. The things my friends did sadden me,

I was in shock when I arrived at my new residence on Wilcox Street. I cried while checking the place out. God! What a dump! There are two little bedrooms and an old wooden scratched-up floor. What a dump! There is no shower, carpet, garbage disposal, fireplace, or beautiful Bay water to play in. This old house was just another dump next to the ghetto. The school was right down the street and looked like how I visualized it. It looked like a prison I once saw in a magazine. I cried for a few weeks and was disturbed by what had happened. I had lost everything. I would pray at night, and I felt as if I were alone, abandoned, and afraid of what my future would bring. What happened, God? All the things I prayed for were taken away."

The government released a mentally ill person on me. The government gave this madman a tool to make me a slave. Now, the government has taken my beautiful home away. What happened, God? Am I just collateral damage?

"God, I only turned thirteen a few months ago, and yet I'm forced to walk in the shadows of others.

TO BE CONTINUED

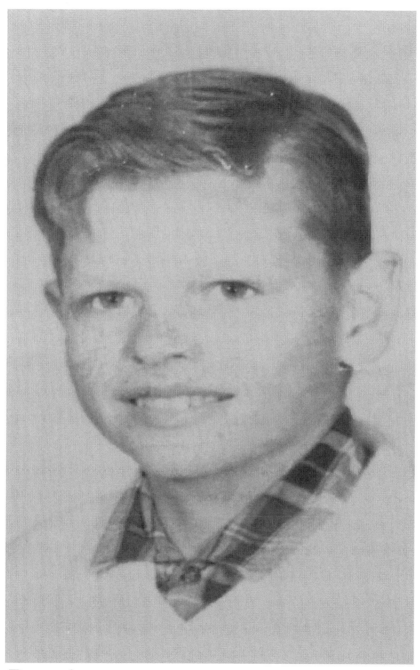

Ronnie age 13

Made in the USA
Las Vegas, NV
25 May 2024